Jewish Ethics as Dialogue

Jewish Ethics as Dialogue
Using Spiritual Language to Re-imagine a Better World

Moses L. Pava

JEWISH ETHICS AS DIALOGUE
Copyright © Moses L. Pava, 2009.

First published in 2009 by PALGRAVE MACMILLAN® in the
United States—a division of St. Martin's Press LLC, 175 Fifth
Avenue, New York, NY 10010

Where this book is distributed in the UK, Europe and the rest of
the world, this is by Palgrave Macmillan, a division of Macmillan
Publishers Limited, registered in England, company number 785998,
of Houndmills, Basingstoke, Hampshire RG21 6XS.

Palgrave Macmillan is the global academic imprint of the above
companies and has companies and representatives throughout the
world.

Palgrave® and Macmillan® are registered trademarks in the United
States, the United Kingdom, Europe and other countries.

ISBN: 978-0-230-61888-6

Library of Congress Cataloging-in-Publication Data

Pava, Moses L.
  Jewish ethics as dialogue : using spiritual language to re-imagine a
better world / Moses L. Pava.
    p. cm.
  Includes bibliographical references and index.
  ISBN 0-230-61888-X (alk. paper)
  1. Jewish ethics. 2. Conduct of life. 3. Dialogue—Religious
aspects—Judaism. 4. Spiritual life—Judaism. 5. Wealth—Religious
aspects—Judaism. I. Title.

BJ1285.2.P38 2009
  296.3'6—dc22   2009013909

A catalogue record of the book is available from the British Library.

Design by Scribe Inc.

First edition: September 2009

10 9 8 7 6 5 4 3 2 1

Printed in the United States of America.

To Vivian

CONTENTS

PREFACE

Each of the nine chapters that constitute the body of this text can be read independently of the others. Nevertheless, it is my hope and aspiration that, taken as a whole, this book reflects a unique perspective on Jewish ethics. While the vision projected in these essays is a deeply personal one that has evolved over the last decade, it is grounded in both traditional and modern Jewish texts.

My overarching goal in these chapters is to demonstrate to the reader the contemporary importance and usefulness of Jewish ethics and values in the modern world. I seek to show here, as in my earlier work on Jewish ethics, that religious and spiritual values can be incorporated into both personal lives and into contemporary organizations in a way that respects individual autonomy, pluralism, democracy, and a deep respect for other moral traditions.

While this book will be of interest to Jewish readers, I believe it will also be of help to everyone struggling to find an appropriate way to access deeply held religious values and spirituality in their everyday lives. The book includes analyses of several Talmudic texts, but no prior knowledge of these texts is assumed.

At their best, these chapters provide a model for an appropriate and legitimate integration of religious and secular aspirations. Although written from inside the Jewish tradition, the goal is to demonstrate to everyone, both inside and outside this tradition, a path of meaning, purpose, and balance. The book will have served its purpose not if it convinces readers to follow my path, but only if it helps readers forge their own vision of what it means to live a life of integrity and connection with others in today's world.

Specifically, this book is built on three major themes. First, imagining Jewish ethics as a kind of dialogue is an authentic, useful, and fertile way of conceiving of what it is we're doing when we're doing Jewish ethics. This dialogue can be thought of as an internal conversation that one has with oneself, but more importantly it is through the give and take with others, the back and forth *flow of meaning*, that the content and authority of ethics is established. It is by remaining in the space of dialogue that we learn about ourselves and others and *together* craft a workable and practical vision of the ethical life and the responsibilities such a life entails. This is the theme of the first three chapters of this book that together make up Part I.

In the first chapter, the basic case for conceiving of Jewish ethics as dialogue is put forth and defended. In the second chapter, attention is focused specifically on how to use traditional language to meet the needs of contemporary ethical problems and failures. This chapter examines the use of *moral imagination*, one of the most important topics in modern ethical theory. Imagining Jewish ethics as dialogue suggests that ethics is more art than science. This issue is taken up in the third and final chapter of Part I through an extended analysis of an important essay by Rabbi Joseph B. Soloveitchik titled "Confrontation." Rabbi Soloveitchik's essay represents one of the most important and often cited discussions of dialogue in modern Jewish thought and provides a useful framework for thinking about the appropriate contours and boundaries for dialogue.

The second major theme of this book, explored in Part II, is that an appropriate and workable view of Jewish ethics for the contemporary world entails a new and more pragmatic view of spirituality than a traditional one. This emerging view, with its worldly focus, complements and grows out of the conception of Jewish ethics as dialogue. Its point is not necessarily to participate in God's inevitable unfolding over time (as others have defined spirituality), but rather it is a process which—by design—culminates in a change in character and in the achievement and satisfaction of an ever growing set of human needs. This view of spirituality is based primarily on the path-breaking views of the American philosopher John Dewey.

Chapter 4 explores the use of spirituality in today's modern purposive organizations. Chapter 5 provides a personal account of the ups and downs of teaching about spirituality in an undergraduate business ethics course. An appendix to Chapter 5 includes an open letter to my students. Chapter 6 represents a response—written from a point of view that openly endorses more (and not less) spirituality in the public sphere—to four new and quite challenging books promoting atheism and decrying religion and religious thought. The goal of this chapter is not to argue with these atheists, but to enter into a dialogue with them.

Finally, the third major theme of this book is that Jewish ethics can help inform, in a healthy and constructive way, public policy discussions concerning major issues confronting democracies across the globe. While this theme appears in both Parts I and II of this book, it is taken up directly in Part III. Chapter 7 critically evaluates Thomas Friedman's flat world metaphor and suggests that such a metaphor, while useful for some purposes, fails as an adequate conception of the emerging global economy. From the point of view of Jewish ethics as dialogue, Friedman's metaphor is severely limited and troubling.

The main thesis of Chapter 8 is that the pursuit, acquisition, and disposition of wealth are all activities that gain their ethical legitimacy as part of a larger, ongoing society-wide dialogue. To use biblical language, we can say that wealth is a necessary good when it promotes, extends, and deepens covenantal responsibilities. When wealth and the power that comes with wealth are misused to cut dialogue short, to engage in strategic communication, or to undercut democratic institutions that support open and free dialogue, wealth and power have exceeded their appropriate boundaries.

Lastly, Chapter 9 warns the reader that despite the great strength and practical utility of thinking of Jewish ethics as dialogue, there exist several important limitations to dialogue as a way of "doing" ethics. We ignore issues like the unfair distribution of power and other trenchant criticisms of dialogue at our own peril. At best, dialogue produces good-enough, uncertain, temporary, and contestable outcomes dependent on the environment and the context in which ethical norms are actually realized.

David Bohm, one of the most important advocates for more and better dialogue in public life, once wrote about dialogue as follows:

When one person says something, the other person does not in general respond with exactly the same meaning as that seen by the first person. Rather, the meanings are only *similar* and not identical. Thus, when the second person replies, the first person sees a *difference* between what he meant to say and what the other person understood. On considering this difference, he may then be able to see something new, which is relevant both to his own views and to those of the other person. And so it can go back and forth, with the continual emergence of a new content that is common to both participants. Thus, in dialogue, each person does not attempt to *make common* certain ideas or items of information that are already known to him. Rather, it may be said that the two people are making something *in common*, i.e., creating something new together. (Bohm 1996, p. 3, emphasis in original)

In embracing dialogue, we jettison hopes for a perfect, single, unchanging answer to our ethical quandaries. All we can really do is go back and forth with one another, understanding one another only imperfectly. What Bohm is suggesting, however, is that it is precisely these imperfections, these errors that allow us to grow, develop, and learn together. I find this to be a truly optimistic and hopeful vision. In thinking of Jewish ethics as dialogue, we are being asked to sacrifice a certain kind of false certainty. We are being asked to take on additional responsibilities, to take ownership of our ethical world. There are no guarantees that we will succeed in this project, but to the extent that we can learn together how to communicate to one another both within and across communities of meaning in an open and noncoercive way, we do have some reason for optimism.

PART I

JEWISH ETHICS AS DIALOGUE

CHAPTER 1

THE CASE FOR DIALOGUE

Ben Zoma said, Who is wise? He who learns from every person, as it is said, From all my teachers I have acquired understanding.

—Avot: 4,1

Through the Thou a man becomes I.

—Martin Buber, *I and Thou*

There exists a class of decisions—I would suggest a large, growing, and important class—that are ethical in nature but do not lend themselves to easy, traditional answers. These are decisions with no single "correct" solution, although almost certainly there are better and worse ones. These questions are not the kind that can be answered once and for all through rabbinic fiat. In fact, in most of these cases, invoking rabbinic authority is itself inappropriate and, at times, deeply problematic from an ethical point of view. I am thinking primarily about political, business, and organizational decisions in pluralistic settings, but this category includes personal choices as well.

Unfortunately, decision makers often resolve such issues without formally recognizing their ethical aspects. At best, ethics is smuggled in, camouflaged in an unarticulated fashion. In other cases, it functions, but only at an unconscious level.

In organizational life, decision making is almost always translated into purely rational terms. What are the benefits of a particular course of action? What are its costs? While these rationalistic techniques—precise and systematic—can be useful and do play an important role in decision making, they are also flawed and limited, especially when it comes to matters of ethics.

Rational decision making breaks down, almost imperceptibly, precisely when it is most needed. When the environment is ambiguous, time is limited, preferences are uncertain, ethics are in play, beliefs are tinged with doubt, and our very identities are on the line, the rules of rational decision making often become more of a hindrance than a help. How can I pick and choose from alternative actions and outcomes if my own preferences are evolving and maturing? Rational decision makers usually ignore issues related to community, justice, aesthetics, culture, and education. If something cannot be measured precisely, from the purely rationalist's point of view, it is simply not "real." Sometimes, this is a useful simplification, but at other times, it can lead to disaster.

Now, if it is true that ethical language plays little or no role in modern, organizational life, this holds all the more for ethical language derived specifically from traditional religious sources. Keeping religion out of political and business decision making does have its merits, of course. Organizational leaders and decision makers avoid religious arguments and unwinnable disputes. When it comes to ethics, the stakes are high, but when it comes to religion, the stakes are perceived as ultimate. If all of us agree to separate completely organizational decision making from religion's intrusions, efficiency is enhanced (perhaps dramatically in many cases), and religion's purity is maintained.

This separation, however, leads to a split between our actions (both public and private) and our core values. This split has grown wider and become more uncomfortable to live with in recent years. Many are beginning to question the wisdom of the status quo. If there exists a disconnect between what we might call our values-in-use and our espoused values, is there anything we can do about this? Is it still possible, in the twenty-first century, to live a life of integrity and integration? These are serious and difficult questions, and they deserve our careful attention.

The Return to the Text

In the Jewish community, the standard response to this problem has been the call for increased text study. Across the United States and Israel, there has been a dramatic growth in the number and quality of Jewish classes being offered at various institutions (synagogues, universities, schools, Jewish Community Centers, federations, businesses, law offices, etc.). There are classes available for all ages, on a wide variety of topics, from preschool to retirement. In addition, there is a huge increase in the number of classic Jewish texts that are now available in English translation. There is little doubt that there is a strong thirst for Jewish knowledge and that there has been a real and substantive revival of Jewish learning across denominations over the past decade.

Unquestionably, text study is a necessary step in reducing the gap between actions and values, but unfortunately, it is insufficient to the task. *Jewish values do not live in Jewish texts.* Jewish values are not fixed propositions embedded in written form that can be easily handed off from one generation to the next. Jewish values are necessarily the product of contemporary Jewish minds. If they are embedded anywhere, they are embedded in our daily actions and in the institutions we help to create through leadership and participation.

The study of ancient and modern Jewish texts, while necessary, can become a substitute for our own original thinking. In fact, text study can be a way of avoiding personal responsibility, a way of hiding from reality rather than facing it squarely. I remember vividly, from my own days in Yeshiva, learning about the precise distinction between *p'shat* (the literal meaning of the text) and *d'rash* (the homiletic meaning of the text). We spent days and days trying to uncover the most likely meaning of a single Talmudic passage. We spent little or no time, however, trying to discover or invent the significance of the passage to our own lives as students, citizens of a democratic country, future professionals, or business leaders (other than in a strictly *halachick* or legalistic fashion). Was it presumed that we were able to take this step on our own? If so, this was a faulty premise.

Text study does not go far enough if it does not engage and challenge students (of any age) directly. What do I (we)—the student(s) reading the text—think about all of this? Is this really something that I (we) can buy into? If so, how can I (we) put the value projected in this text into action? The question is not simply, What do these words mean? but How do I (we) relate to this meaning, if at all? In traditional text study, it is as if we belong to the text. But is it possible for us to reverse this relationship and for us to take ownership of these texts?

BEYOND TEXT STUDY TO ETHICAL DIALOGUE

The thesis of this introductory chapter and the entire volume is that contemporary Jewish ethics requires more than mere text study. It is my belief that Jewish ethics, like all ethics, is the result of ethical dialogues. I put this more formally as follows: It is through the flow of dialogue that the contents of ethical norms are generated and their power and authority is legitimated.

These ethical dialogues can take on numerous forms. They can be highly formalized in organizational, communal, educational, or political settings, or they can be more free-floating. They may be conducted for a short period of time, or they may be ongoing. We may agree to strict rules of engagement (although these rules are themselves subject to dialogue and reconsideration), or we may edge in and out of a dialogue. We may participate in a dialogue through an exchange of e-mails, or I might submit a letter to the editor of my local newspaper. These kinds of dialogues take place in boardrooms, legislatures, universities, schools, synagogues and other institutions.

These dialogues require that we listen to one another in a deep way. We must learn to hear the music beneath the words. They require that we speak openly and candidly to one another and that we stop viewing communication solely as a kind of game that one either wins or loses. Ethical dialogue demands that we remain open to the possibility of learning and growth. We may come out of an ethical dialogue as a different kind of person or as a different kind of community than as we entered. We may embrace new values through the process of dialogue just as we may jettison old ones. We must learn to tolerate silence as well as noise.

Ethical dialogues will never result in perfect, permanent, certain solutions to ethical problems. At best, they will generate good-enough, temporary, and probable solutions, but solutions to which we are accountable because we have agreed to them in a fair process. Ethical dialogues cannot provide a final resting place or a God's-eye view; however, they can provide an opportunity for all of us to speak together from the heart and to be confident that we are being listened to.

One cannot participate in such dialogues strategically, surreptitiously, or in an unthinking way. They require an openness, a tolerance for divergent views, and a new level of self-consciousness and awareness about the central importance of ethics to our lives. If in the past, ethics has gone unarticulated, then ethical dialogues provide an antidote. Decisions driven by unconscious desires must be examined, and to the extent possible, understood for what they are.

Typically, Jewish learning stops after we are convinced that we have finally understood the original intention of a biblical verse or chapter. "This is what they (Rashi, Rambam, Ramban, etc.) meant." The class is finished when we can summarize the point of a particular Mishnaic law or custom. We may ask ourselves how one historical statement articulates with another one. We may follow the historical development of a particular *mitzvah* over time. What we rarely do, however, is confront ourselves with our new knowledge. We forget or are afraid to ask ourselves the all important question, so what? As long, as we can "finish" one page of Talmud per day, what else can anyone ask from us?

We must learn to pick and choose and to have the courage to take responsibility for our choices. Not all historic Jewish values are still credible. Some (everyone is created in the image of God) are better than others (if a husband suspects his wife of adultery, she is forced to drink from the bitter waters). In ethical dialogue, we cannot hide behind the mantle of accepted authority; rather, we must learn how to speak for ourselves.

We must also be prepared to admit that not all of our most cherished values are Jewish in origin. Perhaps the most important issues we are facing are the still very open questions of whether or not democracy, tolerance, feminism, and pluralism are Jewish values, after all. To most of us (including me), the answers seem as self-evident, but to many (especially those most familiar with ancient Jewish texts), these questions are, at best, highly debatable. These questions, though, cannot be answered with recourse only to historical texts. These are the kind of questions that must be answered through open and fair dialogue among those informed by Jewish history, schooled in tradition, and who still care enough to raise the questions and debate their significance to how we live our lives today.

THE NEAR IMPOSSIBILITY OF REMAINING IN THE SPACE OF DIALOGUE

We must learn together how to initiate and maintain dialogues. This requires trust, skill, persistence, and hard work. Although I believe it does make sense to talk about internal dialogue (a dialogue one has with oneself), the kind of dialogues from which legitimate ethical norms and values flow require a confrontation with and a mutual turning toward an other or others. In order to begin to reconnect our espoused values and our values-in-use (i.e., our beliefs and our actions), we must re-create communities and institutions in which this process is openly recognized and encouraged. We must come to learn how to tolerate, respect, honor, and even love those who are different from us.

There are many compelling reasons to promote ethical dialogues, not least of which is the possibility that our very survival as a species may depend on this kind of communication. Nevertheless, ethical dialogues are fragile constructions and are easily shattered. There are several forces, working both independently and together, that can undermine and destroy dialogues. Worse yet, these forces can transform dialogues into dangerous caricatures that can, over time, annihilate our very faith in the possibility of ethical dialogue.

Given the dark shadows of these many forces, is it really possible to remain in the open space of authentic dialogue? The following is a catalogue of some of the many obstacles.

Power

Power, of course, is not evenly distributed among individuals or groups. If I have more of it than you do, why should I engage in dialogue? After all, by definition, I can already get you to do what I want you to do. And, if I do decide to engage in dialogue, isn't it just a strategic game? On the one hand, if I can get you to agree with me without the use of power, so much the better. On the other hand, if our dialogue breaks down (i.e., you still do not agree with me even after I have explained what it is that I'm going to do to you), I still have recourse to my power.

At the extreme, I may threaten (explicitly or implicitly) the use of violence against you. In turn, these threats may lead to the actual use of violence. The one thing I cannot tolerate under any circumstances is a loss of control.

And, if I have *less* power than you, I am surely aware of this fact and the strategic games to which I might be subject. I am taught, usually by those in power, to base my decisions on trust, but surely this advice itself may be part of the game. Power, especially the more unevenly it is distributed, thus becomes an extremely destabilizing factor in both starting and maintaining authentic dialogues.

Fear and Rage

Fear and rage are universal (or nearly so). Most of us harbor a deep fear of one another. We fear our closest intimates, at times. Why else are we so embarrassed to admit certain facts about ourselves to them? We fear our neighbors. What do we really know about them? How much more so do we fear strangers, foreigners, and especially our sworn enemies?

Perhaps we even fear our own selves. How many times have I neglected writing in my private journal for fear of what I might discover about myself if I truly wrote from the heart?

The kinds of ethical dialogues I am advocating demand openness, self-confidence that we will say the right thing at the right time, toleration, honesty, patience, and respect, but can we overcome our fear? And should we even try to overcome our fear? After all, some paranoids are probably correct in assuming that everyone is out to get them.

There exists a rage, a free-floating rage, at the injustices we all suffer. A first cousin of fear, rage is hard to contain within the bounds of civil discourse. I may discover that not only do I not love you, but if I'm true to my own feelings, I also must confess that actually I hate you. Or, perhaps, on second thought, I love you *and* hate you, I admire you *and* resent you—all at the same time.

It just might be the case that I choose to play the charade of dialogue as a way of inflicting punishment on you. Dialogue might be a tool for ethical growth, but it may very well transform itself into a clever tool for my revenge. I will feign openness and honesty to set a trap for you in order to execute my personal version of justice.

Lack of Courage

You may truly want to engage with me in dialogue. But I can never know this with certainty. I may also want to truly engage with you in dialogue. But I resist because of a lack of courage. What if this *is* all a trap? What if I'm afraid that what I have to say isn't important enough? What if I communicate my deepest wishes to you only to be mocked and humiliated, or worse yet, just simply ignored? Do I have the courage to remain in the space of dialogue and tolerate this kind of potential pain? Maybe, maybe not.

Apathy

The flip side of fear, rage, and lack of courage is apathy. I may not even care about ethical dialogue the way you do. I may think all of this time we spend talking to one another and reading one another's e-mails, letters, and essays as a grand waste of my precious time. I may participate from time to time in dialogue, but only out of a vague sense of social courtesy. I may remain in the space of dialogue, but only as a ghost. Dialogue is endless and hopeless from this point of view.

Lack of Respect

It is true that we are not all created as equals, or so one might begin to imagine. If I do not respect you, I certainly do not need to hear what you have to say. Related to lack of respect is a kind of knowingness. I don't need to listen to you because I already know what it is that you are going to say even before you say it.

Lack of Time

Decision making must be timely, and dialogues are notoriously time consuming. They often do not lead to any agreements or clear resolutions. In the face of real or perceived time constraints, leaders must be decisive and let the chips fall where they may. This is perhaps the single most common reason for terminating ethical dialogues.

Uncertainty

Uncertainty creates almost intolerable anxiety. Traditional authoritarian leaders describe and promise a type of ethics that provides followers a sense of security and a certainty. If you do a, b, and c, you will surely receive d, e, and f as your rewards from the gods. Advocates of ethical dialogue can make no such promise.

In fact, it is precisely because we have recognized that all claims to final security and certainty are false that we embrace dialogue as a good enough possibility for survival and growth. But for those unprepared or not ready to accept uncertainty as a fact of life, ethical dialogues are much less appealing, if not downright terrifying.

Unwillingness to Compromise

When it comes to ethics, compromise is a dirty word. As I have described ethical dialogues above, though, they require a willingness to compromise, a willingness to sacrifice—on occasion—one's own deepest values in the name of development and growth. We must be willing to trade up on our values. Sacrifice is, of course, a word with deep roots in traditional religious thinking. It is a concept that might be worth reinterpreting and made appropriate for the modern world. From a traditionalist's point of view, however, it is seemingly impossible to move beyond a literalist equation of sacrifice with the ancient practice of the slaughter of animals for ritual purposes.

I know of no other ethical theory that makes this demand on individuals. According to traditionalists, authentic values must, by definition, be unchanging and constant over time. Once a value, always a value. According to the utilitarians influenced by Jeremy Bentham, one value is as good as another. The notion of higher and lower values is mistaken. Followers of Immanuel Kant (deontologists) believe that personal values must be overcome in arriving at a truly ethical decision. They speak of the categorical imperative as a principle out of time and out of place.

Is it possible that we can self-consciously alter our own evolution? While many of us may believe this to be the case, many others believe that this is a utopian and dangerous dream.

Unconscious Desires

One does not necessarily have to be a Freudian to recognize the reality of a kind of death wish or, if that is too strong of a term, a desire—perhaps unconscious—to undo the good that we have accomplished. Doesn't everyone, on occasion, engage in actions that serve to undercut their professed goals? What is it that we really want? Ethical dialogue may provide one way for building, strengthening, and broadening the circle of community, but it may also provide a convenient location and opportunity to destroy and uproot community. Scarier still, no one is necessarily doing this fully aware of what it is that we are actually doing to ourselves and to others.

KEEPING THE CONVERSATIONS GOING

> In this turbulent time, we crave connection; we long for peace; we want the means to walk through the chaos intact. We are seeking things that are only available through an experience of sacred. Yet sometimes in pursuit of these goals we flee from people and withdraw into an environment we think we can control. Or we blot out our longings with mind-numbing experiences or substances. But we cannot find connection, community, and peace by withdrawing from the other or going unconscious. The peace we seek is found in experiencing ourselves as part of something bigger and wiser than our little, crazed self. The community we belong to is all of life. The turbulence cannot be controlled, but when we stop struggling and accept it as part of life, it feels different. (Wheatley 2002, p. 135)

Power, fear and rage, lack of courage, apathy, lack of respect, lack of time, uncertainty, unwillingness to compromise, and unconscious desires constitute an important list of the forces working against dialogue, but it is still partial. Nevertheless, this list reminds us powerfully of the near impossibility of remaining in the space of dialogue. But these negative forces constitute only part of a bigger story. Let's look at the other side. Just as there is a set of forces pulling us apart (centrifugal forces), there is a second set of forces pulling us together (centripetal forces). From where is the energy generated to keep the conversations going?

We Are Social Beings

We are, at root, social beings. I agree with the psychoanalyst Stephen Mitchell, who wrote, "We are not animals first and then social; we are profoundly, deeply *social animals*" (2002, 66). He continues in a description worth quoting at length:

> Human beings form relationships; we create and preserve linguistic communities. Why? Are communities and the linguistic communication that knits them together the products of discrete needs, perhaps basic drives? No. It is much more than that. Defining humans as relational is quite different from specifying gregariousness or sociability as a specific drive among other drives, like the need for food or the need to reproduce. Consider an analogy.
>
> Human beings are oxygen-breathing organisms; we are not *driven* to seek oxygen (except if it is suddenly withdrawn). It is simply what we are built to do, and we do it without trying to do it or doing it as a means to other ends. Human beings are also language-generating creatures. In the heyday of behaviorism, language was assumed to be an instrumental act that emerged in the individual for some purpose, because it was reinforced. Now language is generally regarded as an *emergent* property of the human brain . . . Human babies generate sounds, and eventually language not for some instrumental purpose, but because they have human brains, and that is what we humans have been designed, over the course of evolution, to do.
>
> We are designed, in many, many ways we are just beginning to appreciate, to be drawn into interaction with other human beings, and these interactions are necessary for babies to be able to use their brains to become specifically human, language-generating creatures, with specifically human minds. (66–67; emphasis in original)

We might add to Mitchell's quote that just as these human interactions are necessary for babies to develop properly, so too are they necessary for children, adolescents, and adults to continue their development. As

Martin Buber tersely put it, "Through the *Thou* a man becomes *I*" (1958, p. 28)

In this view, dialogue is not a luxury we can do with or without, but dialogue is as necessary as the air we breathe. It is, in part, for dialogue that we are designed. No matter how bad things seem to get, somehow we all tend to hold on to this belief, however precariously. Even in our darkest moments, full of ourselves, full of our own fear and rage, certain in our own righteousness, and lacking any kind of real faith, we know in our heart of hearts that it is to dialogue that me must turn, if only we knew how.

Ben Zoma Said . . .

"Who is wise? He who learns from every person, as it is said, *From all my teachers I have acquired understanding*." It is a truism that no one of us is as smart as all of us. When faced with difficult ethical decisions, we lack experience, knowledge, and know-how. At best, we see things only from our own point of view.

It is through dialogue that we attempt to overcome our own egos. Dialogue is a bridge we build together as we walk over it. It is not something we build at once. We hesitate, we begin, we get frustrated, and we may temporarily stop. But we start again; we *must* start again. We recognize that in the long run there is no alternative to dialogue. In the long run, power and violence are unstable and faith in magic is impractical. Power and violence beget more power and more violence. Faith in magic is a giving up. For the pragmatists who continue to believe that some actions are better than others, what we do does make a difference to the quality of our lives, dialogue is our best and last hope.

In Dialogue, Everything Is in Play

The only way to overcome power, rage, fear, and lack of courage is to acknowledge them. At the deepest level, ethical dialogues must confront these issues head on. These negative, centrifugal forces must become the subject of dialogue. We cannot assume equal access to power, nor can we simply bracket off the powerful emotions and desires that drive and motivate so much of our decision making and our behavior. Unless we are allowed to openly talk about power inequalities, our conversations are misleading and false. They generate inauthentic norms.

Why is it that there is a split between our actions and our core values? What drives the seemingly growing gap between values-in-use and our espoused values? These questions themselves must be put to the test of dialogue. When it comes to Jewish life, some of these are hard and unpleasant questions to even raise, let alone to answer. Consider some of the following hypotheses that might explain the split between actions and core values:

1. The ancient Jewish values don't really speak to our current ethical dilemmas. Using Jewish values is like trying to use a hammer when what we really need to solve our problem is a computer.
2. The Jewish values do speak to our ethical dilemmas, but as we try to implement them, we discover they are not very practical to implement.
3. The Jewish values do speak to our ethical dilemmas and they are practical, but they are inappropriate in an organizational context where not everyone is Jewish.
4. Jewish values are authoritarian in nature. In today's modern world, we are being challenged to take responsibility for our actions and to be accountable for them.
5. We really do believe in Jewish values, but there are other conflicting values that we hold as well. These values usually trump our Jewish values.
6. We don't really believe in Jewish values at all. Our Jewish values are part of our imaginative life. We identify with them, but we do not really use them. They serve ornamental purposes but not utilitarian ones.
7. Our values must necessarily change and grow over time as our environment evolves. It is not easy to think of Jewish values in this way. We are afraid that if we think of Jewish values in this way, the values will no longer be Jewish (and neither will we).
8. Jewish values represent an integrated whole. Some would say Jewish values are perfect. Using these values in the real world, however, will force us to compromise them. So, to protect the purity of our values, we leave them at home.

I do not raise these hypotheses because I know for sure whether they are true, partially true, or false. I identify these hypotheses because, in the interest of moral progress, we must begin to talk about these issues in a serious way.

When asked whether or not we believe if there exists a unique set of Jewish values, almost all of us raise our hands, high and proud. Intuitively, we know that Jewish values connect us to our history and help form our very identities. Despite this, however, when it comes to real decision making, when the stakes are high, we will also acknowledge, more hesitantly and less proudly, that it is difficult, if not impossible, to identify and incorporate these unique Jewish values into our public and our private lives. This itself must be a subject of dialogue. Unfortunately, by focusing exclusively on text study to the neglect of dialogue, these hypotheses go unstated and unexamined. It is almost as if we don't really want to know why there exists a gap between actions and professed values.

The Process of Dialogue is a Good in Itself

I believe that one of the strongest forces pulling us toward one another is the recognition that not only do dialogues lead to preferable outcomes (which they do), but dialogues also are good in themselves. Anyone who has ever participated in a real dialogue comes to appreciate the process for its own sake. One exits a dialogue not tired and apathetic, but excited and hopeful.

In fact, ethical dialogues teach us that the sharp distinction we make between process and outcome (means and ends) is merely a more or less useful tool for decision making. It is one way we choose to organize our world with the hope that it helps us to improve our lives. But the distinctions we make are at best temporary and practical. It may make perfect sense to specify that certain actions are only a means to creating a particular kind of world. But we forget that these actions themselves are part of this very same world we are in the process of creating at our own peril. As we observe ourselves in the moment of decision making, we recognize means *are* ends, if only temporarily, and ends *are* merely means to even more distant ends.

It is interesting to discover what one has in common with others, just as it is interesting to discover how different each of us is. In the theory of rational decision making, preferences and desires are assumed to be fixed and unchanging. In dialogue, new preferences and new desires begin to emerge. We learn new facts, not only about the world and each other, but also about ourselves, as well.

Ethical dialogues provide an opportunity to express our own creativity. In a nonjudgmental and supportive atmosphere, we can be playful and innovative. Imagination and logical consistency are both valued and promoted through this process.

Dialogues promote fairness, transparency, and lead to more and better accountability. In fact, the very notion of accountability—being able to explain my actions to those most affected by them—presumes a context of dialogue.

Re-imagining Covenant

At the heart of traditional Jewish ethics is the idea of covenant. It is a truism to note that the idea of covenant or *brit* is deeply rooted in the rich soil of biblical narrative. Not only is it is a term that describes the climactic events of Sinai, but it also is a term that echoes through every book of the Bible. Covenant is the central organizing theme of biblical thought.

For the purposes of developing a full-blown Jewish ethics, we need to provide a contemporary definition consistent with traditional Jewish sources but compelling enough to help move us forward to face the emerging challenges of the new century. I define it, formally, as a voluntary agreement among independent but equal agents to create a "shared community." The primary purpose of the agreement is to self-consciously provide a stable social location for the interpretation of life's meanings in order to help foster human growth, development, and the satisfaction of human needs.

This definition is meant to highlight three aspects of *brit*. First, covenants are purposely ambiguous and open-ended, thus allowing for change and growth. Second, they are long term in nature. And third, covenants are respectful of human integrity.

These kinds of covenants (and there may be as many covenants as there are human purposes) must necessarily be built and sustained by ethical dialogues. The notion of dialogue is not necessarily original to Judaism (as perhaps the notion of covenant is), but dialogue is consistent with Judaism's most fundamental values. It is a necessary step to help bridge the gap between our deepest beliefs (core values) and our everyday actions.

ETHICAL DIALOGUE AS A
WAY INTO THE ORGANIZATION

If we are to reduce the gap between our beliefs and our actions, we must necessarily find a place for religious values in our modern, purposive organizations. Much of our waking lives are spent inside such organizations and to ignore our deepest values for so much time seems like too much to ask from us. Yet, we must tread very carefully here because religious values are so often promoted in coercive and unfair ways. Values derived from religion are often authoritarian in nature and lack democratic legitimacy. Furthermore, such values may be parochial in nature and favor one group over another for no other reason than one is a member of a particular religion.

The gap between beliefs and action is not only a problem for the individual to face alone. In fact, I believe the gap is primarily an institutional problem, and therefore it requires institutional solutions. This is an important reason why the study of ancient texts (Jewish or otherwise), while necessary, is really insufficient as a solution. No amount of personal study or personal commitment to religious values will fully resolve the problem we are talking about in this chapter.

This is why the promotion and implementation of ethical dialogues becomes so timely and important. An ethical dialogue can never be the result of a single decision maker acting alone. By definition, dialogues belong to institutions and to communities of people. They must be conducted in open and transparent ways.

Ethical dialogues of necessity require respect for differences, a new and deep kind of listening, and a willingness to grow and develop through contact with those whom we disagree (at least, initially). At the same time, these dialogues demand each and every one of us to speak with our own authentic voice. For many of us, of course, this means we will need to invoke a vocabulary derived from religious sources. Are such dialogues really possible? I believe that the answer to this question is yes. Furthermore, it is this belief that constitutes the common thread that ties together the remaining chapters in this volume.

CONCLUSION

This chapter has built a case for altering our understanding of Jewish ethics. Instead of viewing ethics as contained in a book or a text, it is useful to conceive of Jewish ethics as part of an ongoing dialogue. I have identified what I consider several of the benefits of ethical dialogue. At the same time, I have admitted many of the seemingly overwhelming difficulties in engaging in authentic dialogue. I have not attempted to "prove" that the positive forces outweigh the negative ones, nor that the benefits of ethical dialogues outweigh their costs. I certainly do not contend that ethical dialogue is inevitable.

My point is to put forth a vision, warts and all, that I believe is worthy of contemplation and experimentation, one day at a time. It is my faith that we can reasonably affect outcomes in the world in which we all live in a positive way, but we hardly possess all of the answers. Even under the best of circumstances, we must talk together and choose actions wisely, modestly, and humbly. We must be continuous learners, ready to admit our mistakes and start over (again and again), and we must somehow find the energy to persist.

James March, one of the leading experts in the world in decision theory, once concluded rather pessimistically that the world is "absurd." In my darker moments, I almost agree with this negative conclusion, but I prefer Martin Buber's formulation: "The world is not understandable but it is embraceable; through the embracing of one of its beings." I don't think we should read Buber's intention solely as referring to a physical embrace here. He is talking about a broader kind of spiritual, emotional, cognitive, *and* physical embrace—a kind of embrace that results only from dialogue with others.

This chapter suggests that we need to recognize our own responsibility in imagining and forming Jewish values. I am afraid this admission of our own hands in all of this is not something that makes us very comfortable. It is much easier to simply accept a set of inherited Jewish values and piously pledge allegiance to them. We boast, "Our acceptance of these values is what makes us who we are—it is what makes us Jewish." The problem though is that even as we pledge our deepest allegiance to these values, to be honest we also must admit that we do not really use them to guide our behavior. Is there a way to become self-conscious about this? Is there anything we can do to bridge the gap between our professed values and our everyday actions? To answer these questions in the affirmative demands a combination of realism and moral imagination. It is to these topics that we turn to in the next chapter.

CHAPTER 2*

INCREASING MORAL CAPITAL THROUGH MORAL IMAGINATION

Traditional Jewish communities are beginning to recognize an increasingly obvious crisis in the area of applied ethics. This is not a sociological investigation, so no attempt will be made to document this problem in a systematic way. I will begin simply by citing three extreme examples of ethics failures inside traditional Jewish communities. These are highly emotional issues, and they raise questions about the very identity of the Jewish community.

First, the last decade has seen numerous allegations of lapses in business ethics. Many of these stories are well known, and I will not elaborate on them here. Second, the murder of Yitchak Rabin by a young man who claimed to act out of religious convictions should have provided the impetus for a deep soul searching in religious communities, but never did. Third, the allegations of sexual, physical, and verbal abuse of children against a former employee of the Orthodox Union's National Conference of Synagogue Youth who was well known and respected by many North American orthodox communities is perhaps the most difficult failure of all to fathom. The kinds of charges that were being levied against this individual and the organization that employed him deserve careful and balanced scrutiny. Each of these examples reveals unexamined problems inherent in traditional Jewish communities. It is my opinion that, taken together, these examples suggest a crisis.

This chapter is primarily directed to those of us who already recognize these unfortunate situations as a cause for grave concern inside the traditional community. It is an attempt to formulate, if not a solution, then a least an optimistic case for the future moral viability of traditional communities. The chapter is written from the perspective

*An earlier version of this chapter appeared in *The Edah Journal* 2, no. 2 (2002): 2–11.

of an involved and responsible insider looking out—at least, that is the aspiration. It is an attempt to consider this crisis in an authentic and honest way, in a way that takes both tradition and the contemporary world very seriously. This chapter will be successful not only if you agree with my conclusions but also if it helps to jump-start a dialogue about who we are and where we are going.

The Quest for Ethical Leadership

I begin with a definition of ethical leadership. Ethical leadership means using the moral language that belongs to all of us. Ethical leaders learn this language and apply it uniquely and creatively to solve emerging human problems. This definition of leadership can be put more starkly (if slightly less accurately) as follows: *Ethical leaders use yesterday's language to solve tomorrow's problems.* In doing so, ideally, they both solve the problem and expand our language.

No one—not even the greatest and most innovative leader—can create a complete and private language. In fact, when we consider what language is and what it is for, it dawns on us that a private language is a contradiction in terms. Leaders, like everyone else, always emerge from community and, first of all, absorb its traditions and existing language. All of us begin life's journey by seeing our way through the eyes of the community. Perceptions are filtered through its vocabulary and grammar.

But, as one matures, new and confounding problems inevitably present themselves. They can arise in any number of ways; they can emerge from within or be imposed on us from without. At first, many of these new problems seem so different from our earlier ones. Often, however, they are not. And, one is reassured by the tradition and its defenders that there is nothing new under the sun. What looks new on the surface turns out to be an old and familiar problem. One is correctly taught, as a first step, to reframe the new problem and solve it using the trusted language and techniques of the past.

Many seemingly intractable ethical problems can be solved in the same exact way we answer apparently complex mathematical problems. While I cannot solve *this* algebraic equation, I can solve *that* algebraic equation, and it turns out that *this* algebraic equation can be cleverly transformed into *that* algebraic equation.

Easy and Hard Cases in Ethics

Ethical problems that can be transformed in this way—and almost all ethical problems have to be tweaked at least a little—make up the *easy* cases, or at least, the relatively easy cases. A kind of "ethical technology" is useful in solving such cases where standard rules and procedures play the most important roles. Easy cases fit with the assumptions of the rule book. You figure out what kind of case you're faced with and you apply the appropriate predetermined rule to solve the dilemma.

Not every ethical problem is easy, however. Sometimes, the honest decision maker must admit to herself that this really is a *new* situation. Conditions have changed, technologies are altered, and values evolve. While a new situation shares some of the characteristics of the old cases, it doesn't share enough of them. There is often no recognizable pattern. Capturing the new problem with the old language seems like putting a square peg in a round hole.

It is even difficult to talk about or to describe the underlying ethical issue because our language lacks an appropriate and rich-enough vocabulary. Existing language is not always adequate to solve the problems we ask from it. Just as a community that has never encountered an exotic bird before would have no name for it, a traditional community that has never faced the problems of citizenship in a legitimate democracy before would have no words to express the dilemma precisely, let alone resolve it. Whenever there is a gap between our language and our world, we face a *hard* case in ethics.

The Temptations of Fundamentalism and Moral Miserliness

Fundamentalists deny the possibility of this kind of a gap. According to this view, one never openly admits that there are hard cases in ethics. I think a good definition of fundamentalism is the a priori rejection of new problems. To the fundamentalist mind, the idea that there is nothing new under the sun is not only good, prudent advice to use as a first step in approaching new problems, but it also becomes an essential element of one's faith. It becomes not just the starting point, but the final resting place as well.

In such situations, fundamentalists exhibit two choices. The first option is to ignore the essential defining elements of the new problem (i.e., those characteristics that make the problem different from the old problems) and to continue to apply the strategy of reframing. In this view, all ethical problems are easy cases.

In my work in Jewish business ethics, I have come to see that this is a familiar strategy among contemporary rabbis. Instead of dealing with real problems faced by actual managers in modern organizations, rabbis "solve" highly stylized, but more familiar problems. As an extreme example of what I mean by reframing, I remember vividly asking a well-respected orthodox rabbi about a corporation's social responsibilities to employees and local communities. The rabbi said he could not answer this question, even if it is one of the most important issues in contemporary business, because the *Shulkhan Arukh* does not recognize the existence of corporations as a halakhic category. Instead, he proceeded to deliver an hour lecture on whether or not a bar mitzvah boy has to pay taxes on his gifts (by the way, according to this rabbi, he is not obligated by *halakha* to pay even if the government does require such payment). Unfortunately for our community, many rabbis prefer to rehearse the answers to yesterday's questions rather than answering the relevant questions that today's community is posing.

A second option for the fundamentalists, and even more radical than the first, is to simply ignore the new problem outright. The convoluted logic here runs as follows. I am certain that my existing language is perfectly complete. If I do not already possess the solution to the problem, there is no problem. While from time to time, all of us succumb to the temptations of this kind of arrogance and intellectual laziness, only fundamentalists suggest that this is the right thing to do! Ironically, fundamentalists like many of the most radical postmodern thinkers (those all the way on the other side of the intellectual continuum), claim that all we have is the text, as if there really was no world out there and no problems in it.

Here is an example. I vividly recall a proposal I once had for a modern orthodox Jewish think tank to examine possible contradictions and connections between traditional religious thought and the intellectual assumptions of the modern social sciences. Economics, for example, assumes boldly and proudly that human beings are best thought of as rational utility maximizers. This pervasive assumption in contemporary economics asserts that *all* decision making is exclusively consequentialist and preference based. The only thing that matters is future outcomes (or consequences), and the only way to evaluate them is through individual tastes (preferences). This decision-making model, far from being a testable hypothesis among economists, provides the very method and foundation for economic analysis today. My proposal included raising the question of whether or not such a method might not be antithetical (or at least problematic and worthy of discussion) from a religious perspective founded on the idea that man is created in God's image. It might be especially problematic from a Jewish perspective that insists on explicitly linking all-important decisions to traditional and authoritative texts. In addition, I suggested that there may be similar problems in other areas of social science (e.g., psychology). I did not raise these issues because I think we need to abandon economic analysis or jettison religious language. Quite to the contrary, the point was to see if we could find some commonalities and begin an honest process of integration. The proposal was immediately shot down, I was told, because such a proposal might uncover problems for which the religious community does not yet have the answers. Better to shut our eyes and pretend the problems don't exist than to raise new questions without certain answers in hand, a nearly perfect expression of the fundamentalist worldview.

What drives this willful blindness on the part of fundamentalists is, I think, an understandable desire to preserve moral capital. Fundamentalists are justly concerned that once we begin to play with language and to purposely manipulate it for our own interests, we risk the possibility of irreparable damage to the language that, quite literally, defines us. The obvious flaw here, however, is that fundamentalists completely ignore another kind of risk, at times much more dangerous, which is inherent in their decision to cut themselves off from continuing to examine the world and how it actually works. In short, this second risk suggests that those who ignore the world will face eventual exposure to the likely possibility of evil.

Those who ignore the living world and the problems it throws at us are, in time, almost certainly doomed to extinction. In a world where there is a significant possibility of evil, ignoring it simply because one doesn't have a name for it is not only careless but also unethical. This is especially true for those in a position of leadership in the community where others are relying on the wisdom and advice of the leader. In their zealous attempt to guard and protect the tradition, fundamentalists turn their back on the future and face rearward. It is almost as if they are driving a car facing the back window rather than the front.

Fundamentalists are *moral misers*, always refusing to borrow from the moral capital to build a better future. In treasuring their inherited language and traditions, they miss their point entirely. In a literal sense, they begin to idolize the language, as if human language was itself a God.

While fundamentalism is not a viable option, there is something important for us to learn and take from it. Fundamentalists are right in claiming that preserving moral capital is the first principle of ethical decision making. In order to maintain and ensure our identity over time, moral arguments must be self-consciously grounded in traditional language. Herein lies the great strength of their position. This principle suggests that our *ethical decisions must always respect the integrity of moral language.* At the end of the day, the moral language is all we have to help resolve ethical predicaments. The fundamentalists are right when they insist that making it up as we go along is incoherent and self-contradictory.

ACCEPTING THE WORLD AND REJECTING FUNDAMENTALISM

The necessary rejection of fundamentalism, however, suggests the existence of a second principle. This principle can be formulated simply: *Respond to the real problems in the real world.*

There is an independently existing world out there, and it can wreak havoc on us unless we attempt to understand it. (Of course, even if we do understand it, there may be nothing we can do about it.) But, it is an irresponsible and immoral naiveté to willfully blind oneself to one's surroundings simply because one cannot readily understand the environment given one's current ideals, values, and language. This violates the second necessary principle of ethical decision making.

There are gaps between our language and our world, which is to say that there are hard ethical cases to resolve, whether we like it or not. To move beyond fundamentalism and to avoid nihilism, we need a process of decision making and a theory to undergird it that allows us to integrate the two principles identified above.

A key step in moving out of fundamentalism lies in the recognition that language is not static. Language is dynamic. Like people themselves, languages can mature and grow, or wither away and die. Or, putting the same idea in slightly different words, it is a deep and fatal philosophical and religious mistake to believe that there exists a fixed amount of moral capital.

MORAL SPENDTHRIFTS

In facing and resolving the hard cases in ethics, there is a risk that we will eat into our moral capital, the shared stock of practical and human wisdom embedded in language and tradition.

I would suggest, however, that in extreme cases, expending moral capital is the morally correct decision to make. There are extreme situations where, in the short run, more weight is correctly assigned to the second principle rather than the first. There are real-world problems that require us to knowingly abuse (temporarily) the integrity of language in order to satisfy immediate survival needs. Here, Immanuel Kant, the justly famous moral philosopher, was wrong to think that lying is prohibited in every conceivable case. It is not only permissible to lie to an intruder who would kill an innocent person, but it also is the ethically correct action. Kant was correct that, in the long run, lying will undercut the very possibility for truth, but in the short run it may very well be the lesser of two evils. To be sure, one must do this with extreme care, and, even as one damages the language, one should be aware of the damage and try to do so in the least offensive way.

I think it is possible and necessary on occasion to expend moral capital. But, at the same time, one must avoid becoming a *moral spendthrift, one* who continually draws on moral capital but never makes any new deposits. If this is true, it must make sense to say that one can replenish or even enhance and increase moral capital. If one rejects this possibility, then we are stuck without hope between the miserliness of fundamentalism on the one hand, and the eventual bankruptcy of moral language on the other.

MORAL IMAGINATION: AN INVESTMENT IN MORAL CAPITAL

As stated above, sometimes a hard case in ethics is so hard that it requires us, in the short run, to violate temporarily the first principle. If this is the decision, we try to implement it in a way that causes the least amount of permanent damage. In addition, on occasion, we may choose to set aside resolving a problem and coming to a final conclusion when it is not life threatening and the cost to integrity of any conceivable solution is judged prohibitive.

The difference between this prescription and fundamentalism is that here, if we do choose to "ignore" a problem—today there is no conceivable way of resolving this problem without permanently destroying the integrity of our language—we still keep conscious track of the problem as best we can. In other words, we attempt to "account" for the problem even if we cannot finally "solve" it. There is a huge difference in admitting there is an unresolved problem and insisting on engaging in an ongoing search for a resolution versus pretending that the problem does not exist in the first place.

A good example of this kind of agnosticism, again taken from the business ethics literature, can be found in a paper by Michael Broyde and Stephen Resnicoff. This example provides a stark contrast to the Rabbi alluded to above. In a rich, long, and winding discussion on the modern corporation and Jewish law, the authors finally conclude, "None of the Jewish Law theories of a corporation is entirely satisfying or compelling" (Broyde and Resnicoff 1999, 272). Some authors might have ignored the tough and intractable questions and issues raised in this paper altogether because there is no final bottom-line resolution on the topic. The authors put aside a final decision even while they do an admirable job of keeping track of the problem. One might consider Broyde and Resnicoff's well-documented admission of uncertainty an admirable and courageous step beyond fundamentalism toward moral development, especially considering the context in which the paper was delivered. (In the past, another invited paper at this forum was rejected outright because some of the members felt the conclusions the author drew violated basic tenets of orthodoxy.)

It is not the final step, however (in ethical decision making, there is no final step). Some hard cases in ethics are, in fact, resolvable in a way which does not require a trade-off between the two principles cited above. On occasion, we can resolve an altogether new ethical problem by respecting the moral integrity of language, even while we are responding to the actual problem that confronts us. I would go further, though. Not only can we resolve the problem, but the resolution itself also may enhance or *increase the moral capital*. This process of resolving hard cases in ethics in a way that increases moral capital requires something called moral imagination.

The idea of increasing moral capital requires one to reject the certain belief that our existing moral language is perfect. A perfectly complete and final language in an evolving and changing world is incoherent. In order to use yesterday's language to solve tomorrow's problems, leaders must find a legitimate way to alter yesterday's language without destroying it.

In dealing with hard cases in ethics, the question finally boils down to this: How does one change the language while preserving its integrity? Notice that it is not a question of whether or not it is permissible to change the language, but rather the better and more interesting question is *how* is such change enacted in an authentic way? In answering this broad question, it is useful to consider each of the following more specific ones:

1. *The Question of Importing*: Does the reasoned choice of incorporating elements of foreign languages into one's native language necessarily violate integrity?

2. *The Question of Responsible Choosing*: Does self-consciously ignoring elements of one's native language necessarily violate integrity?
3. *The Question of Inventing*: Does one necessarily violate integrity when one attempts to invent new vocabulary by building on the old vocabulary?
4. *The Question of Interpreting*: Is integrity violated necessarily in the search for new meanings inside the old language?

Advocates of moral imagination answer each of these questions with a resounding "no." In fact, importing, choosing, inventing, and interpreting constitute the tasks of moral imagination and provide the mechanisms for moral growth. This is not to say, of course, that *all* importing, choosing, inventing, and interpreting are legitimate in the context of every existing language. It is simply that each case of importing, choosing, inventing, and interpreting must be examined on its own merits.

The Question of Importing

No one language is perfect. Or, as we are often correctly reminded in myriads of ways, no one of us is as smart as all of us. When it comes to moral capital (as opposed to financial capital) taking from others should be encouraged and not discouraged. "What is mine is mine and what is mine is yours" holds for everyone in the case of moral capital. Languages that have developed and evolved under differing historical circumstances will embed a diversity of truths. One of the great benefits of language is that one does not have to learn every lesson the hard way. If I am smart, I can listen to you and capitalize on your experiences. The better one listens to others, the more one learns. In short, often the easiest way to use yesterday's language to solve tomorrow's problem is to realize that there are other legitimate languages out there. Martin Luther King Jr. learned ethical lessons from Gandhi, and Gandhi claimed that he imported elements into his own nonviolent philosophy from the early American philosopher, Henry David Thoreau. In recognizing pluralism, one takes a first step toward a practical solution to hard cases in ethics.

How can importing be of practical use to the orthodox community? The leadership of the Orthodox Union who allowed Baruch Lanner to continue leading youth groups for a period of twenty-seven years, even after a series of independent accusations of child abuse had been made against him, should have immediately adopted the policies of other organizations and groups that had faced similar problems in the past. Accusations of child abuse against an employee are indeed examples of hard cases in ethics. Instead of trying to institutionalize a program of sexual conduct appropriate for National Council of Synagogue Youth (such codes of conduct are easily available for adaptation), the leaders at the Orthodox Union continued for some time to claim ignorance of the problem.

Further, there is an inherent strength in importing from other languages. Borrowing, although it can only begin if we admit that there are differences between languages, can actually help to convince us that the differences are not as large or insurmountable as we might have first thought. Borrowing is a practical way to solve our hard cases in ethics and increase our moral vocabulary. In addition, borrowing has the collateral benefit of helping to enlarge—or at least build bridges between—moral communities.In solving a hard case in ethics through importing, the very notion of what makes up "our community" is put into play. It may turn out, at the end of the day, that our community is larger, more expansive, and more complicated than we originally thought. As moral capital expands, the idea of community is altered as well.

For two distinct reasons importing, however, is not always a viable option. First, it may turn out that importing does violate the integrity of one's own native language. It is easy to think of cases where borrowing a concept or a term from another language *would* undercut basic axioms of one's own position. The point here is merely that it is not always and forever the case that importing violates integrity. Second, importing may not be viable because no existing language may have the vocabulary to solve a new problem. The fact that we do not have a solution to a hard case does not mean that some other language does. Nevertheless, even with these two major limitations in mind, importing is a powerful and profound way to increase the moral capital. Here, I merely cite the work of the medieval philosopher Moses Maimonides and his justly famous *The Guide of the Perplexed* as the single most important example of this approach within Judaism. In fact, much of the original controversy surrounding the approach of Maimonides focused on the legitimacy of importing in Judaism.

The Question of Legitimate Choosing

In looking at the question of importing, the notion of pluralism becomes important where pluralism suggests the existence of many different moral languages coexisting at a point in time. Pluralism also helps us think through the question of legitimate choosing. Can one legitimately pick and choose from within one's own language? If one's language reflects only a single coherent voice, then I think the answer to this question would, in fact, be no. However, to the extent that languages themselves are pluralistic or perceived to be pluralistic (i.e., they reflect more than one single voice), then the very attempt to make the language coherent requires one to pick and choose.

It is not easy to solve a hard case in ethics. There are situations where an ethical leader in using yesterday's language is going to have to make difficult choices. He or she may willfully ignore part of the tradition when that element of the tradition is seen as the cause of the problem in the first place. I wonder if some of the Rabbis who openly encouraged Yitchak Rabin's murderer considered the possibility that some of the textual resources they were exploiting simply should have been ignored as inappropriate in the context of a modern democracy.

When great leaders pick and choose with care and attention in the face of difficult choices, moral capital is increased. The next generation inherits a language that is better suited to solving ethical dilemmas.

The Question of Inventing

Fundamentalists who continue to assert the perfection of the inherited language are, of course, opposed to the possibility of invention. With a perfectly complete moral vocabulary in hand, invention can only harm and can never help. On the other hand, if hard cases in ethics truly exist, invention may turn out to be a legitimate tool to enlarge the moral capital.

How do great leaders invent? First of all, it is important to keep in mind that invention is not creation out of nothing. Inventors— whether one is talking about inventors of mechanical or electronic gadgetry or ethical inventors—use the materials at hand. The genius of invention is always in how one puts those preexisting materials together. Invention requires experimentation and the willingness to put up with temporary failure. When Thomas Edison invented the lightbulb, he did not magically produce something entirely new out of thin air. His genius, as he was the first to insist, consisted almost entirely in his patient quest to find the best material to use to produce his filament, in spite of numerous false starts.

But, if invention is not creation out of nothing, what is it? The best way to think about creation is as a kind of integration. The dictionary defines integration as the process of "making into a whole by bring- ing all parts together." I think there is more to it, though. I define integration as *the process of uncovering new relationships among discrete elements from which new value emerges.* Rabbi Norman Lamm, the former president of Yeshiva University, is surely correct when he notes that today we no longer view organic unity as a fact, but as a value to be pursued consciously in human life and civilization. In other words, integration is not a state of being to be taken for granted, but a valuable human process. Integration is something that reasonable people can do, and integration is something that reasonable people have good reasons to do. Restating this using theological language, Lamm proceeds boldly: "The unity of God is, unquestionably, not yet a fact; it must await . . . eschatological fulfillment. But that fulfillment must not be merely a passive one, relegated only to the heart. If not (yet) a fact, it must be championed as a value. It must motivate an active program so that all of life will move toward realizing that 'And the Lord shall be king over all the earth'; that the 'World of Disintegration' will one day be replaced by the 'World of Unity' and reintegration" (Lamm 1998, 65). In Lamm's hands, unity becomes a goal to be pursued rather than a description of current reality. The whole of being is *not yet* one individual, but there is a religious and moral duty to come to see the world in this way. Integration is not passive, but active.

Viewing invention in this way, it is hardly of the "make it up as you please variety," but becomes a core element of moral imagination. In Jewish business ethics, Hillel's innovative and integrative reading of Deuteronomy, against the backdrop of what he perceived as a hard case in ethics, led him to invent his famous *prosbul*, a legal document that effectively allowed lenders and borrowers to circumvent the biblically mandated cancellation of the debt in the sabbatical year, and to thus ensure the healthy growth of the economy. This is exactly the kind of innovative thinking our community needs today to help resolve business ethics dilemmas but it is almost totally absent in contemporary discussions of Jewish business ethics. The one notable exception is our community's justifiable pride in Aaron Feurestein's well-publicized decision to continue paying his idle employees while a burned down factory was being rebuilt.

The Question of Interpreting

The behavioral scientist James March has astutely observed that sometimes decision making is not about deciding what I, or we, should do today, but it is better envisaged as rethinking the meaning of what we did yesterday.

Decision making shapes meanings even as it is shaped by them. A choice process provides an occasion for developing and diffusing interpretations of history and current conditions, as well as for mutual construction of theories of life. It is an occasion for defining virtue and truth, discovering or interpreting what is happening, what decision makers have been doing, and what justifies their actions. It is an occasion for distributing glory and blame for what has happened, and thus an occasion for exercising, challenging, and reaffirming friendship and trust relationships, antagonisms, and power and status relationships. Decision and decision making play a major role in the development of the meaning and interpretations that decisions are based upon. (March 1999, 27)

The basic idea here is that from time to time (when one is faced with a hard case in ethics), in order to move forward, we must retrace our steps and reconsider the meaning of our past accomplishments and failures. In other words, there may yet be new meaning embedded in the old language. From the perspective of the fundamentalists, the question of interpretation is the most controversial of all. From this perspective, meaning is something that is thrust on us, once and for all.

Great moral leaders, faced with hard cases, cannot afford such overly pious beliefs. Great leaders challenge us to rethink the meaning of our lives and communities. Here, one can cite Abraham Lincoln's imaginative reference to the "real" meaning of the phrase "all men are created equal" at a time of political and moral crisis. His example, I think, demonstrates the possibility of increasing moral capital—not by abandoning moral language and making it up as you please, but by finding new and better meanings inside old and well-accepted language.

This idea is well illustrated in Jewish sources by rethinking one of the most important stories in the entire Bible. Consider the famous biblical narrative of Abraham and the binding of Isaac. This story, as related in Genesis 22, is traditionally understood as an example of "blind obedience" to a Divine command. A careful reading of the biblical narrative, however, suggests an altogether different reading.

In verse 2, the literal translation of the text states that God commands Abraham to "lift Isaac up as an offering." Abraham's initial interpretation of the Divine imperative is that God is asking for a human sacrifice, and, as Abraham begins his three-day journey to the "mountain which I will tell thee of," Abraham is willing to obey. Abraham is predisposed to such an interpretation. In the environment in which he grew up, child sacrifice was considered the ultimate act of faith and piety. Had Abraham actually slaughtered Isaac, his contemporaries would have considered him a great Canaanite religious leader. To Abraham, however, this was not sufficient.

Through an act of moral imagination, Abraham burst onto the world stage for posterity. With knife in hand, "Abraham lifted up his eyes and looked" (Genesis 22:13). And what did Abraham see? He saw "a ram caught in the thicket by his horns." Abraham's genius resided in the fact that he finally recognized that he could fulfill the literal interpretation of God's command and demonstrate his ultimate devotion to God even as he replaced Isaac with a ram. The Bible recounts, "and he offered the ram up for a burnt offering instead of his son." In a sense, this is the true climax of the story. When the angel speaks to Abraham and warns him not to "harm the lad," it is not a new commandment—God does not change his mind—but it is the original commandment interpreted in a better and more ethically sensitive way. In recognizing that a ram can symbolically take the place of his son, Abraham demonstrates the power of creative interpretation and the revolutionary implications of the path of moral imagination. Abraham does not reject the commandment and become a superman; rather, Abraham becomes a better and more authentic version of himself and thus provides a model for all ethical leaders who follow him. He solves a hard case in ethics. He avoids the temptations of fundamentalism and sidesteps the trap of moral bankruptcy. Most importantly, for present purposes, he increases the moral capital. Abraham understood that his case was a hard case. In solving it, he transformed it into an easy case for all his followers.

In this chapter, I am asserting that there exists a crisis in traditional Jewish communities. In short, the kinds of problems that our community faces today simply did not exist in the past. The good news is that we can solve these problems. But to do so, we must become more self-conscious about importing, choosing, inventing, and interpreting. Those of us who see this need first must have the courage to talk about it publicly, even at the risk of upsetting the fundamentalists.

Conclusion

To summarize the discussion—great leaders use yesterday's language to solve tomorrow's problems. How so?

Great leaders distinguish between easy and hard cases. Easy cases may require a reframing of a problem, but in reframing, one recognizes that the seemingly new problem bears a striking resemblance to old problems. Old problems can be resolved through old language.

If there truly is a new problem, ethical leaders have three options. One, they can temporarily violate the integrity of their inherited language (this is always a last resort). Two, they can avoid making a decision, even while they continue to monitor the problem and search for a solution. Or three, they can engage in a process of moral imagination that will include importing, choosing, inventing, or interpreting (or, of course, some combination). The long-run benefit of moral imagination is the possibility for the growth of moral capital. Of the three possible options outlined here, moral imagination is the only *necessary* option for solving hard cases in ethics. I suggest that all three of the examples with which this chapter began require Jewish leaders and all members of the community to apply moral imagination in a judicious way in emerging ethical dialogues.

My major conclusion for the present purposes is that all of this is good news for those of us involved in areas of applied ethics. There is an "ethics of authenticity," as the philosopher Charles Taylor so aptly put it in his slim but important book by that name. Taylor suggests that, authenticity, correctly understood, "(A) involves (i) creation and construction as well as discovery, (ii) originality, and frequently (iii) opposition to the rules of society and even potentially to what we recognize as morality. But it is also true that it (B) requires (i) openness to horizons of significance (for otherwise the creation loses the background that can save it from insignificance), and (ii) self-definition in dialogue. That these demands may be in tension has to be allowed" (Taylor 1991, 66). Taylor's description of an "ethics of authenticity" in dialogue emphasizes the human aspect in all of this. His is neither a prescription for moral miserliness nor moral bankruptcy. He recognizes our modern predicament and offers a plausible way out. There are no final guarantees here, but at least authenticity promises some hope. For those of us involved in Jewish ethics, or any religiously grounded system of ethics, this chapter is a suggestion to try it. Our claim of constituting a moral community is at stake.

In emphasizing the concept of moral imagination, this chapter has implied that ethics is as much an art as it is a science. In the next chapter, this implication is examined in detail.

CHAPTER 3

THE ART OF ETHICAL DIALOGUE

When we give ourselves over to loving somebody, it is not just them we are discovering and loving but who we are and who we will become when we are with them.

—Stephen Mitchell, *Can Love Last?*

But of the religious attitude which is allied to acceptance of the ideally good as the to-be-realized possibilities of existence, one statement may be made with confidence. At the best, all our endeavors look to the future and never attain certainty.

—John Dewey, *The Quest for Certainty*

An ethical dialogue is a special form of communication between two or more human beings. The purpose of an ethical dialogue is to self-consciously cocreate an imaginary space between us, a safe place we enter or leave at our own choosing. It is a bounded space reserved for playing with serious ideas. It is where we come together to speak honestly and openly, without fear of rebuke or retaliation. It is where you and I come to accept and appreciate the wholeness of our world, learn more about ourselves, and reach agreements about how best to live our lives together.

It is not only a space where information is traded between us, but it is also where ideas, ideals, desires, stories, dreams, and memories are invented and shared. Unlike "normal conversations," in ethical dialogues we begin to "explore underlying causes, rules, and assumptions to get to deeper questions and framing of problems" (Isaacs 1999, 41). Through such generative dialogues "unprecedented possibilities and new insights" emerge (ibid). Borders between us are negotiated and renegotiated. It is a place where I recognize your uniqueness and you recognize mine, and in this mutual recognition our essential equality is established.

An ethical dialogue is something that we choose or choose not to construct together. It is like a fine crystal goblet: both valuable and extremely fragile. It is like a covenant: freely entered, open-ended, and respectful of human differences. The space of dialogue provides a stable-enough location for the interpretation of life's meanings. It is here that human growth is self-consciously fostered, the bonds between us are examined and strengthened, and the satisfaction of some of our deepest desires and needs are temporarily satisfied. *It is through the flow of dialogue that the contents of ethical norms are generated and their power and authority is legitimated.*

Ethical dialogues take place at many different levels. They can take place in the bedroom, consulting room, classroom, and boardroom. They are located in intimate conversations, op-ed pages of newspapers, books, journals, movies, songs, and poems. They are conducted in schools, universities, churches, synagogues, mosques, national legislatures, and world congresses. Some ethical dialogues are formal and regulated, while others are spontaneous and unplanned; most fall somewhere between these two extremes.

The contents of ethical norms generated through dialogues are *always more or less ambiguous and open-ended* and subject to further interpretations and more intensive dialogues. The best results we can hope for are likely, probable, tentative, and temporary. Further, the power and legitimacy of these norms are always uncertain and subject to question. These observations, emphasizing the human responsibility in creating ethics, tend to make us anxious. One often longs to forget them and yearns for something more definitive and permanent, a kind of lodestar beyond and above earthly limitations.

Human history is littered with attempts to foist one's own deeply felt, certain and clear, understanding of ethics onto the other—and almost always it is the wealthier and the more powerful individuals and groups that are doing the foisting. While these attempts are advertised variously as necessary, natural, divine, certain, objective, scientific, for-your-own-good, and unambiguous, they never are. Ethical norms and values are constructed, understood, and applied by fallible human beings in an uncertain and seemingly indifferent world—a world in which resources are unevenly and arbitrarily distributed, motives are always mixed, and futures are never perfectly scripted.

Does the recognition that we contribute to the production of our own ethics imply that anything goes? Hardly, once we recognize that the texture of how we experience our lives together, and perhaps our very survival on this planet, is a function of the quality of our ethical dialogues.

The quality of these dialogues, in turn, is a function of the intellectual capabilities, education, emotional intelligence, leadership skills, spiritual aspirations, imagination, and motivation of dialogue participants. Quality is a function of history, language, memory, and perceived power relationships. It is a function of what I think you owe me and what I think I owe you (and vice versa). It is a func tion of our reputations for honesty and trustworthiness, and how I perceive what is in your best interest and how you perceive what is in my best interest.

William Isaacs, in his book *Dialogue and the Art of Thinking Together*, writes that there is a point in the dialogue process when "a recognizably different kind of conversation begins to take place. Here the energy changes. People finally stop speaking for others, or for 'the group.' There is a shift from 'third person data'—stories about other people and other places—to 'first person data'—inquiries into how things look from where I stand . . . People are reflective in this phase—about what they are doing, about the impact they are having" (1999, 272). Dialogue participants are no longer trying to win a debate and score points against their opponents, but now exhibit a real curiosity and openness and a deep sense of connectedness. "They discover that there is a larger meaning unfolding through the conversation—something that goes beyond what they might have imagined and constructed for themselves" (ibid). People are no longer worried about whether or not others are agreeing or disagreeing with them. The formal politeness that characterizes some kinds of conversations is surpassed. As the dialogue deepens further, there is often a "letting-go of an isolated identity that many of us have developed and used to survive in the world." We begin to see the heavy losses we impose on ourselves by holding onto our old selves in an unhealthy and unthinking way. "Two people who come together can learn to transcend the limits of their identities and come to the point of knowing a larger sense of destiny together than they might have experienced on their own. In it comes the realization that we are not our point of view, that the shared identity we have had is not what we thought, and that we can together see more than we might have on our own" (ibid, 279).

Beyond this stage of reflective dialogue exists an even more profound transformative quality of talking and reasoning together. "It is the one where people cross over into an awareness of the primacy of the whole" (ibid). Isaacs labels this generative dialogue. Truly new ways of looking at the world unfold through the flow of dialogue. There is a "release of structures that limit the flow of meaning" (ibid, 282). One's own voice, previously fearful, isolated, and silenced because of a lack of words to express itself authentically, is found and unleashed. In this kind of dialogue, one discovers something reminiscent of Elijah the prophet's "still small voice"(1 Kings 19:12) perceived only after the winds, earthquakes, and fires diminish.

THE LONELY MAN OF FAITH

One of the most outstanding descriptions of ethical dialogues in recent Jewish philosophy is found in an important essay by Rabbi Joseph B. Soloveitchik[1] titled "Confrontation" (1964). In a kind of a modern-day midrash, Rabbi Soloveitchik fills in some of the gaps in the creation story in Genesis. Writing with poetic fervor, he imagines the following primal scene:

> There is, however, a . . . level which man, if he is longing for self-fulfillment, must ascend. At this level, man finds himself confronted again. Only this time it is not the confrontation of a subject who gazes, with a sense of superiority, at the object beneath him, but of two equal subjects, both lonely in their otherness and uniqueness, both opposed and rejected by an objective order, both craving companionship. This time the two confronters stand alongside each other, each admitting the existence of the other.
>
> Two individuals, lonely and helpless in their solitude, meet and the first community is formed.
>
> The community can only be born, however, through an act of communication. After gazing at each other in silence and defiance, the two individuals involved in a unique encounter begin to communicate with each other. Out of the mist of muteness the miraculous word rises and shines forth. Adam suddenly begins to talk—"And the man said." He addresses himself to Eve, and with his opening remark, two fenced-in isolated human existences open up, and they both ecstatically break through to each other.

Through an act of communication, in dialogue, a new kind of world, a social world, emerges for the first time. "The miraculous word rises and shines forth," and a bridge between two human consciousnesses is created. "An aloof existence is transformed into a together-existence."

Together with all humanity, we are "committed to the general welfare and progress of mankind" and "we are interested in combating disease, in alleviating human suffering, in protecting man's rights, in helping the needy." For Rabbi Soloveitchik, both liberalism and democracy are taken as self-evident values.

Expanding on the importance of dialogue, not just between two individuals, but also between faith communities, Rabbi Soloveitchik writes as follows: "Religious values, doctrines and concepts may be and have been translated into cultural categories enjoyed and cherished even by secular man. All the references throughout the ages to universal religion, philosophical religion, et cetera, are related to the cultural aspect of the faith experience of which not only the community of believers but a pragmatic, utilitarian society avails itself, as well. The cultural religious experience gives meaning and directedness to human existence and relates it to great ultimates, thus enhancing human dignity and worth even at a mundane level." This is an empowering vision, but it is hardly a vision of anything goes. Rabbi Soloveitchik imposes clear boundaries severely limiting the possibilities of dialogues. In his description, dialogues between human beings must always remain unalterably utilitarian. Rabbi Soloveitchik's "together-existence" is strictly and unambiguously self-regulated. While his is a social view of human life, it entails a community inhabited by the most lonely and isolated of individuals. "Man, in his encounter with an objective world and in his assumption of the role of a subject who asks questions about something hitherto simple, forfeits his sense of serenity and peace. He is no longer happy, he begins to examine his station in this world and he finds himself suddenly assailed by perplexity and fear, and especially loneliness. The I-experience is a passional one and real man is born amid the pains of confrontation with an 'angry' environment of which he had previously been an integral part." In this view, there is nothing in interpersonal dialogue that can overcome this profound and existential loneliness. While William Isaacs envisions a stage of dialogue "where people cross over into an awareness of the primacy of the whole," Rabbi Soloveitchik's worldview is essentially a psychology of radical individualism.

Surprisingly, even in the most personal and intimate relationships between lovers and friends, "the bonds uniting two individuals, the modi existentiae remain totally unique and hence, incongruous, at both levels, the ontological and the experiential." Paradoxically, Rabbi Soloveitchik writes, the better two individuals get to know one another, the more aware they become of the absolute and unbridgeable distance between them.

The following lengthy quotation, I believe, fairly captures the severe limitations of any type of interpersonal, I–Thou relationship:

> It is paradoxical yet nonetheless true that each human being lives both in an existential community, surrounded by friends, and in a state of

existential loneliness and tension, confronted by strangers. In each to whom I relate as a human being, I find a friend, for we have many things in common, as well as a stranger, for each of us is unique and wholly other. This otherness stands in the way of complete mutual understanding. The gap of uniqueness is too wide to be bridged. Indeed, it is not a gap, it is an abyss. Of course, there prevails, quite often, a harmony of interests, —economic, political, social—upon which two individuals focus their attention. However, two people glancing at the same object may continue to lead isolated, closed-in existences. Coordination of interest does not spell an existential union. We frequently engage in common enterprise and we prudently pursue common goals, traveling temporarily along parallel roads, yet our destinations are not the same. We are, in the words of the Torah, a helpmeet to each other, yet at the same time, we experience the state of *kenegdo*—we remain different and opposed to each other. We think, feel, and respond to events not in unison but singly, each one in his individual fashion. Man is a social being, yearning for a together-existence in which services are exchanged and experiences shared, and a lonely creature, shy and reticent, fearful of the intruding cynical glance of his next door neighbor. In spite of our sociability and outer-directed nature, we remain strangers to each other. *Our feelings of sympathy and love for our confronter are rooted in surface personality and they do not reach into the inner recesses of our depth personality which never leaves its ontological seclusion and never becomes involved in a communal existence.* (emphasis added)

Here is a description of a poignant, mournful, and almost hopeless longing for deep companionship, but this longing to overcome our mutual fear is just that—a mere longing. "The gap of uniqueness is too wide to be bridged." The best one can attain between two individuals is a kind of useful comradery. There may indeed exist a temporary "harmony of interests," but "coordination of interest does not spell an existential union." For Rabbi Soloveitchik's lonely man of faith even love is diminished to the point that it is, at best, "rooted in surface personality."

Rabbi Soloveitchik believes that each of us possesses, at our core, a "depth personality." I imagine this depth personality as an impenetrable rock. It is inaccessible to others, permanent, untouched, and unchanging. In its self-sufficiency it has no need to participate in community, nor should it. "God created man and endowed him with individual dignity, He decreed that the ontological legitimacy and relevance of the individual human being is to be discovered not without but within the individual. He was created because God approved of him as an autonomous human being and not as an auxiliary being in the service of someone else."

Human dialogue, in this view, is short-circuited and stunted. Words unite us, but as "miraculous" as they are, they can just as easily separate us. "The word is the medium of expressing agreement and concurrence, of reaching mutual understanding, organizing cooperative effort, and uniting action." But, there are no words and there is no language by which we can communicate our "depth personality" to one another. Interpersonal dialogue will never provide a sense of wholeness because this wholeness is a fiction. It is impossible to create a safe place for ethical dialogue to contain and protect us because nothing should or can fully contain the hard rock of a lonely depth personality

THREE STAGES IN THE PSYCHO-SPIRITUAL DEVELOPMENT OF THE LONELY MAN OF FAITH

A Simple and Natural Man

Rabbi Soloveitchik reads the Genesis narrative as describing human psychological and spiritual development. In the essay I have been analyzing, he discovers three stages or "three progressive levels." In the beginning, man is a simple, natural being.

> He is united with nature, moving straight forwards, with the beast and the fowl of the field, along an unbroken line of mechanical life-activities, never turning around, never glancing backwards, leading an existence which is neither fraught with contradiction nor perplexed by paradoxes, nor marred by fright.
>
> Man who was created out of the dust of the ground, enveloped in a mist rising from the jungle, determined by biological immediacy and mechanical necessity, knows of no responsibility, no opposition, no fear, and no dichotomy, and hence he is free from carrying the load of humanity.
>
> Before him stretches the vast garden with an almost endless variety of trees desirable and good, tempting, fascinating, and exciting the boundless fantasy with their glamorous colors.

According to Eugene Korn, this description is of "the pagan of antiquity and the hedonistic, power-driven aesthete or our time" (14).

Man as a Subject Against Nature

This first stage, however tempting it may appear to some of us, is merely temporary. Suddenly, man senses his own otherness and he becomes a stranger to the environment and to himself. He no longer imagines himself as part and parcel of the natural order of things. Man is now a confronted, responsible, and accountable being. Man's sense of subjectivity emerges in this stage, and "the human tragic destiny begins to unfold." Man is now a self-conscious being. "Man, in his encounter with an objective world and in his assumption of the role of a subject who asks questions about something hitherto simple, forfeits his sense of serenity and peace. He is no longer happy, he begins to examine his station in this world and he finds himself suddenly assailed by perplexity and fear, and especially loneliness." At this level, man is called on to play an active role in the world, to conquer and to subdue it through the intelligent and prudent use of power. The goal, according to Rabbi Soloveitchik, is to "gain supremacy over the objective order."

Interpersonal Man

Finally, through the creation of Eve and the acquisition of human language, man reaches the third stage of human development. Now he is confronted not only with a hostile environment and a mandated responsibility to subdue it, but he is confronted by a fellow human being as well. It is precisely this third stage that I described in detail above.

For Rabbi Soloveitchik's fully mature and lonely man of faith, life is now a constant struggle to protect one's own essence, one's depth personality from the other. It *is* an impenetrable rock, but it is also seemingly under constant threat and attack. The response to such perceived threats, according to Rabbi Soloveitchik, is often to depersonalize the other and turn him or her into an object to be manipulated, to meet power with more power. In order to survive, we wrongly seek to domineer and to dominate our fellow human beings. "He [man] has developed the habit of confronting his fellow man in a fashion similar to that which prevails at the level of subject object relationship [man as a subject against nature], seeking to dominate and subordinate him instead of communicating and communing with him. The wondrous personal confrontation of Adam and Eve is thus turned into an ugly attempt at depersonalization. Adam of today wants to appear as master-hero and to subject Eve to his rule and dominion, be it ideological, religious, economic, or political." At best, for Rabbi Soloveitchik there is a kind of retreat and withdrawal from this over-whelming modern tendency to seek power and control. The best one can hope for is to use one another—openly, transparently, and respon-sibly—for mutual benefit and gain. For real relief, redemption, per-manent comfort, and true interconnectedness, the lonely man of faith turns his attention completely to God. "The great encounter between God and man is a wholly personal private affair incomprehensible to the outsider—even to a brother of the same faith community."

Even if one rejects Rabbi Soloveitchik's psychology, one should avoid the temptation to turn it into a caricature. Rabbi Soloveit-chik's lonely man of faith struggles mightily to maintain a tension between his depth personality and a sense of community belonging and responsibility. He writes, for example, "In a word, the greatness of man manifests itself in his dialectical approach to this confronter, in ambivalent acting toward his fellowman, in giving friendship and hurling defiance, in relating himself to, and at the same time, retreat-ing from him. In the dichotomy of *ezer* [helpmeet] and *kenegdo* [over against] we find our triumph as well as our defeat." This last descrip-tion, in my view, captures important aspects of the human experience. It is true that one is both pulled and repelled by the other simultane-ously. There does seem to be a dialectical moving toward and a mov-ing away from one's fellow human beings. One does often sense a profound kind of loneliness even in the midst of sharing. Friendship is always tinged with defiance and aloofness.

Advocates of ethical dialogue would be remiss if they did not include such insights about the contradictory nature of human per-sonality into a full understanding of both the possibilities and the limi-tations of dialogue. While the process of dialogue, at its best, may help us come to accept and appreciate wholeness, it is a dynamic and com-plex wholeness made up of an infinite number of tiny puzzle pieces.

CAN THERE BE TOO MUCH "RETREAT AND WITHDRAWAL?"

While Rabbi Soloveitchik is correct to note the danger of "seeking to dominate and subordinate" the other, is there not also a symmetrical danger of withdrawing and removing oneself prematurely from the other? In fact, with regard to the second level of development (what I termed "man as a subject against nature"), Rabbi Soloveitchik recog-nizes this problem explicitly. He writes that in his confrontation with the outside world, "man may despair, succumb to the overpowering pressure of the objective outside and end in mute resignation, failing to discharge his duty as an intellectual being, and thus dissolving an intelligent existence into an absurd nightmare." But, might it not also be possible at the third level (interpersonal man) to despair, withdraw, and fail to discharge one's duty to the other?

Describing the second level, Rabbi Soloveitchik carefully notes the individual's need to constantly balance participation against surrender. One has to remain in the space of confrontation—the space between becoming too active or too passive in relation to the objective world. So, too, in the realm of "personal confrontation" (the third level), one might exhibit too much power, but one can also surrender to the other prematurely, give up, or withdraw from the space of interpersonal confrontation too soon. In other words, one may choose to simply pick up one's rock and go home before the game is really over.

As it is formulated by Rabbi Soloveitchik, in the case of personal confrontation, it appears that the only problem one has to worry about is to not overpower and overwhelm the other. In his view, the less power one exerts in personal relationships the better.

There is also a real possibility for too little power and participation at this level. In some cases, we must stand inside the space of confrontation and face the other's power not with more power but with just the appropriate balance of power and surrender. This balance represents a deep *acceptance* of the other. It requires one to overcome his or her fear of being swallowed up by the other or, perhaps worse yet, swallowing up the other oneself.

Even the less powerful partner must own up to a degree of accountability to the other. In withdrawing and retreating back into our own fixed and determinate core selves, we may be unknowingly giving up something of true and unappreciated value. William Isaacs writes, "In dialogues that seem to flow powerfully, people begin to realize that they are speaking to the common pool of meaning being created by all the people together and not to each other as individuals. They are seeking to gather a new quality of meaning and understanding together" (1999, 174). In withdrawing prematurely, the lonely man of faith may miss a unique opportunity for learning and growth.

There is always a risk in the entanglement of human relationships. In dialogue, we open ourselves up to the other and seek recognition. We learn to listen, suspend, respect, and voice (Isaacs 1999). Rabbi Soloveitchik is correctly concerned about opening ourselves up too much to an overpowering other who will abuse us. This is a real and constant threat. Nevertheless, his formulation ignores the other side of this problem, namely choosing not to participate and turning one-self away too soon.

"Our feelings of sympathy and love for our confronter are rooted in surface personality and they do not reach into the inner recesses of our depth personality which never leaves its ontological seclusion and never becomes involved in a communal existence." In this sentence, the tension between self and other is loosened to the point where there is a real danger that the self becomes completely detached and self-absorbed. The dialectic between self and other is not overcome but collapses. What Rabbi Soloveitchik fails to imagine is that in stay-ing in the space of personal confrontation—in the space of ethical dialogue—one deepens his or her own understanding of this "depth personality." At their best, the power, recognition, and surrender entailed by ethical dialogue may be enacted in the protective shadow of appreciation, respect, and deep acceptance. In this way, fear is trans-formed into a real and encompassing love.

It is precisely through more open and free dialogue that one comes to grow and mature as a person. In Rabbi Soloveitchik's formula-tion, the isolated and lonely "depth personality," refusing to share its deepest thoughts and risk the scrutiny of dialogue, prevents itself from growing more complex over time, expanding, or learning to live together with the other more deeply and complexly. Sadly, its own fear becomes a self-fulfilling prophecy. As Emmanuel Ghent noted, the sense of one's own wholeness, paradoxically, is enhanced, not diminished, by the sense of unity with other living beings (as quoted by Benjamin 2005).

Martin Buber wrote in his famous book, *I and Thou,* "Through the Thou a man becomes I" (1958, 28). This is a key and profound insight in understanding how dialogue works, and it is a seemingly missing element in Rabbi Soloveitchik's essay "Confrontation." For Rabbi Soloveitchik, Adam's depth personality is fully formed *before* his encounter with his helpmeet. In true dialogue, one's depth personal-ity engages in a joint process of learning and becoming.

A STAGE BEYOND THE "DEPTH PERSONALITY"

We emerge out of and are saturated with relations with others, yet we (in Western culture) organize our experience into selves with what feel like distinct, inviolable interiors, with boundaries, partly negotiable and partly nonnegotiable.

—Stephen Mitchell, *Can Love Last?*

The "depth personality" is rightly considered a stage of human psychological and spiritual development. It is an attainment and an accomplishment, but is it necessarily a final resting place? In viewing the human story in terms of psychological and spiritual development, Rabbi Soloveitchik's own essay opens up this question. Just as both natural man and man as a subject against nature were ignorant of any greater possibilities for human development (and surely were certain that they had reached full maturity), might it not also be the case that our own hyperindividual depth personality is blind to its own potential for continued growth? Or, is this where an authentically religious view of ourselves—a view firmly grounded in Jewish texts—must necessarily terminate? Is the core depth personality—the solid rock of our identity—an ontological fact of given reality as it so self-evidently seems to us or is it simply a highly useful, but ultimately limited, way of organizing, describing, and thinking about human experiences?

Many psychologists, philosophers, and social critics now accept an alternative description of psychological and spiritual development that goes beyond Rabbi Soloveitchik's insistence on radical individualism. Instead of turning our own subjective personalities into personal idols, we can learn to hold onto ourselves more lightly. We give up an attitude of willfulness in favor of willingness. In taking ourselves more seriously, we view our old selves less seriously and as less brittle.

The psychoanalyst Steven Mitchell is one of the clearest, most consistent, and least equivocal spokespersons for this emerging view of human development. He writes,

It is a hallmark of the shift in basic psychoanalytic sensibility that the prototype of mental health for many contemporary analytic authors is not the scientist but the artist. A continual objective take on reality is regarded as neither possible nor valuable in contrast to the ability to develop and move in and out of different perspectives on reality. The ideal of self-deferential absorption in the study of external reality has been replaced by the ideal of self-expression and self-exploration. The injunction "Know thyself" has been amended to the injunctions

"Express thyself" and "Explore thyself." What is healthy is the capacity to sustain multiple estimations of oneself, different ones for different purposes. (2002, 109)

Instead of possessing depth personalities that are forever fixed, they are thought of as fluid. They are more open and less closed. They are more vulnerable but contain more potential. They are less like rocks and more like sea shells that can be worn or shed as the owner wishes.

Like Rabbi Soloveitchik's lonely man of faith, Mitchell and others view humans as social creatures. For the lonely man of faith (and earlier psychoanalytic views), though, social relations are secondary and external. For Mitchell, "we are not animals first and then social; we are profoundly, deeply *social animals*" (66).

Here is how Mitchell retells the primal story of language and the emergence of human beings. It contrasts sharply with Rabbi Soloveitchik's telling:

> Human beings form relationships; we create and preserve linguistic communities. Why? Are communities and the linguistic communication that knits them together the products of discrete needs, perhaps basic drives? No. It is much more than that. Defining humans as relational is quite different from specifying gregariousness or sociability as a specific drive among other drives, like the need for food or the need to reproduce. Consider an analogy.
>
> Human being are oxygen-breathing organisms; we are not *driven* to seek oxygen (except if it is suddenly withdrawn). It is simply what we are built to do, and we do it without trying to do it or doing it as a means to other ends. Human beings are also language-generating creatures. In the heyday of behaviorism, language was assumed to be an instrumental act that emerged in the individual for some purpose, because it was reinforced. Now language is generally regarded as an *emergent* property of the human brain . . . Human babies generate sounds, and eventually language not for some instrumental purpose, but because they have human brains, and that is what we humans have been designed, over the course of evolution, to do.
>
> We are designed, in many, many ways we are just beginning to appreciate, to be drawn into interaction with other human beings, and these interactions are necessary for babies to be able to use their brains to become specifically human, language-generating creatures, with specifically human minds. (66–67; emphasis in original)

The most important difference between this view of language and Rabbi Soloveitchik's revolves around the issue of whether or not language is merely an instrumental tool. Rabbi Soloveitchik's image is one of a human being that *uses* language for his or her own preexisting purposes, but is not, in turn, *formed* by that very same language. The image is one of a human being who is fully transparent to himself. For Rabbi Soloveitchik, it makes sense to imagine Adam using words to communicate with Eve and having him unilaterally tell her about not only what unites them but also about what separates them, without ever waiting for a response from his partner and actually listening to her. It is no wonder then that "Eve was both enlightened and perplexed, assured and troubled by his word."

Ethical dialogue at the deepest level, however, loosens the idea that we are transparent to ourselves. Judith Butler notes, "Ethics requires us to risk ourselves precisely at moment of unknowingness, when what forms us diverges from what lies before us, when our willingness to become undone in relation to others constitutes our chance of becoming human" (2005, 136). For Mitchell, too, to become specifically human, to possess a human mind, is to be embedded in language. Language and dialogue make us, as much as we make them.

Mitchell never dismisses the idea that there exists an impossible gap between self and other, but what he notices is that to truly know oneself, one must embrace the other. His view does not collapse the dialectic between self and other, but clarifies and sharpens it. "Opposites attract because they are inversions of each other, the same thing in different forms. Otherness, in this way of thinking, might be redefined, not as what is truly alien to the self, but as what has been squelched, truncated, disallowed in the self" (82). For Mitchell, we might say that the lonely man of faith is neither mistaken nor deluded, but his vision is truncated. It is one possibility among others that one may self-consciously adopt, and no doubt, for some purposes it may serve us well.

Rabbi Soloveitchik's lonely man of faith is faced with a conundrum. He possesses a desire and longing to connect with others, but he is afraid that any movement toward or away from others will lead to either overpowering the other or being overpowered oneself. In existential crisis, paralyzed, and uncertain, he turns away from the world and his fellow human beings and toward God, in a private search for certainty, redemption, and assurance. He carves up the world—into private and public spheres, religious and secular spheres, and spiritual and material spheres. These are a legitimate choices, but they are not the only choices available for the lonely man of faith.

The lonely man of faith might have understood that his quest for certainty, redemption, and assurance itself might have been questioned. Perhaps his choice to turn away from the world and his fellow human beings was premature. Perhaps his decision to carve the world in two leads to as many problems as it solves. Perhaps he is less transparent to himself than he imagines. He might have recognized that even if now our vocabulary and language are too thin to express our deepest needs and desires—our core depth personality—he might still be able to invent new ways of communicating, new words, new art, and new ideas, especially if he remains in the space of dialogue together with others. As Robert Grudin writes, "Individual identity can never be fully realized unless it is regularly dissolved into dialogue" (1996, 211).

The lonely man of faith desires certainty and wants to rise above the constant change he is experiencing in this world. This change, according to Rabbi Soloveitchik, is often felt at first as a kind of alluring female beauty and perfection, but ultimately it is experienced as evil.[2] He desires complete security and finality. He harbors a wish to win his freedom from the natural order only to offer "this very freedom as the great sacrifice to God, who wills man to be free in order that he may commit himself unreservedly and forfeit his freedom."

He might have realized, though, that as much as it seems to us that man is *against* nature, it might very well be the case that humans will always be *part of* nature. He might have realized that there is more than one way of knowing the world and each other. For the lonely man of faith, "knowledge is gained only through conflict." But, today, scientists like the world-renowned biologist Barbara McClintock, who studied how chromosomes work, describe a different experience: "When I was really working with them I wasn't outside, I was . . . right down there with them, and everything got big. I even was able to see the internal parts of chromosomes. It surprised me, because I actually felt as if I was right down there and these were my friends . . . As you look at these thing, they become part of you. And you forget yourself" (as quoted by Benjamin 2005). Surprises can be scary, and forgetting yourself can be unsettling. The lonely man of faith senses this and retreats before it is too late. But he was neither compelled nor commanded to do so.

There are stages of human psychological and spiritual development beyond traditionalism that can be described and experienced positively.[3] At these higher stages, self-consciousness, autonomy, and self-authorship become objects of contemplation. Individuals no longer exclusively look to authority figures for legitimacy. The "deep self may now come to the surface to be healed and fulfilled, or at least to be known and lived with nondefensively. If it is not resisted, it may thus lead to deeper trust of the self and also to profound awareness of one's relatedness to others . . . This trust takes the form of a profound, self-aware conviction of interdependence" (Parks 2000, 86). Both/and thinking often replaces either/or thinking. Paradox is explored and celebrated rather than quickly resolved. There is an interpenetration of self and other. The quest for permanence and certainty is finally abandoned in favor of temporary safety and "good-enough" solutions.

These changes are experienced as a kind of sacrifice, but they are not experienced as a moving away from personal meaning and spirituality. In fact, these emerging and novel ways of organizing our world provide the framework for a broadening and deepening of our conception of meaning and spirituality. Spirituality can now be defined as the blending of integrity *and* integration through acceptance, commitment, reasonable choice, mindful action, and continuous dialogue (both internal and external).

A FORM OF "MARRANO WRITING" OR THE PURPOSEFUL EMBRACE OF PARADOX?

Suspending the demand for self-identity or, more particularly, for complete coherence seems to me to counter a certain ethical violence, which demands that we manifest and maintain self-identity at all times and require that others do the same.

—Judith Butler, *Giving an Account of Oneself*

In his recent book *For the Sake of Heaven and Earth*, in a parenthetical aside, Rabbi Irving Greenberg, a leading advocate for interfaith dialogue and a former student of Rabbi Soloveitchik, raises a most interesting proposition with regard to the "Confrontation" essay. He writes, "I judged 'Confrontation' to be a piece of 'Marrano writing' (that is to say, the surface words conveyed one message while the substantive depth expressed a very different meaning)" (2004, 13). Pointing to some seeming contradictions in the essay, Rabbi Greenberg concludes that "if [interfaith] dialogue was permitted in matters of social concern, then it was permitted in all areas" (ibid). Suggesting that Rabbi Soloveitchik was engaged in a form of Marrano writing is an intriguing proposition, a bold move, and not one that I would necessarily take as a first step. Nevertheless, it is a creative and generative idea.

In response to Rabbi Greenberg, I suggest that there is a simpler and subtler hypothesis to consider here. While much of the above discussion assumes an identity between Rabbi Soloveitchik's portrait of the lonely man of faith and Rabbi Soloveitchik himself, this identity need not hold. In fact, a careful rereading of some of the above quotations suggests that Rabbi Soloveitchik, unlike his lonely man of faith, *does* remain in the space of dialogue and *does* openly reflect on many of his deepest thoughts and beliefs, subjecting them in a transparent way to public scrutiny in a far greater way than his rabbinic predecessors, peers, and followers. How many of us would willingly and so poignantly acknowledge our deep fear of the other? How many of us would willingly admit our inability to express ourselves to even our closest companions? Indeed, many of us sense the same loneliness as Rabbi Soloveitchik's lonely man of faith but fail to communicate this loneliness to others as Rabbi Soloveitchik so eloquently does. While it may be true that the lonely man of faith protects his depth personality at far too high a price, this may not be true for Rabbi Soloveitchik's own depth personality. When Rabbi Soloveitchik writes, "Our approach to and relationship with the outside world has always been of an ambivalent character, intrinsically antithetic, bordering at times on the paradoxical," it sounds to me, at quite an explicit level, much more like the postmodernism of Stephen Mitchell and Judith Butler (see the epigraph to this section), than the traditionalism of his own lonely man of faith.

The "Confrontation" essay suggests that there are indeed many real limitations to dialogue, specifically interfaith dialogue. He writes, "In the same manner as Adam and Eve . . . encountered each other as two separate individuals cognizant of their incommensurability and uniqueness, so also two faith communities which coordinate their efforts when confronted by the cosmic order may face each other in the full knowledge of their distinctness and individuality." In the case of interfaith dialogue, Rabbi Soloveitchik (in the body of his text) draws a bright line between the spiritual and secular orders. In his prescription, he allows for, and encourages, interfaith dialogue that focuses exclusively on secular matters, but forcefully prohibits interfaith dialogue that focuses on specifically religious issues. "As a matter of fact our common interests lie not in the realm of faith, but in the realm of the secular orders." But, in perhaps the most astonishing aspect of this essay, Rabbi Soloveitchik attaches endnote 8 to this sentence, which seems to undercut the essential distinction he has just made. To the text, he appends, "The term 'secular orders' is used here in accordance with its popular semantics, for the man of faith, this term is a misnomer. *God claims the whole, not a part of man, and whatever he established as an order within the scheme of creation is sacred"* (emphasis added). This leads, though, to an obvious question. If indeed "the term secular orders is a misnomer," then how is it that the man of faith can in good consciousness use this very distinction as his fundamental guide in conducting interfaith dialogues? This is one of the major contradictions that Rabbi Irving Greenberg identifies as evidence suggesting that Rabbi Soloveitchik is writing to two distinct audiences simultaneously, an elite audience of his informed peers and a more traditionally-minded group of rabbinic colleagues.

Reuven Kimelman agrees with this conclusion. He notes, "The essay constitutes a meditative ambivalent reflection on the complexity of the issues. Its contradictory quality is intrinsic to its message . . . It thus serves as a prohibition for the many and a permission for the few." Kimelman immediately continues by noting that "some will claim that the Rav [Rabbi Soloveitchik] is talking out of both sides of his mouth." Rather than denying this claim, Kimelman states, "Precisely; the fragmented modern Jewish situation prevents a single answer on the burning issues of the soul" (2004, 9).

My suggestion, however, is that rather than writing *to* two audiences, he is writing *from* two alternative psychological perspectives. From one perspective, there is a certainty and clarity about one's own personality and ultimate aims. It is a perspective that emphasizes autonomy, authority, logic, right and wrong thinking, an obvious demarcation between the religious and secular spheres, and clear and unchangeable boundaries between self and other and between us and them. From the alternative perspective, authority is a construction, right and wrong are sometimes ambiguous, there is an intermingling of the religious and secular spheres, and the other is a mirror of the self. Michael Walzer seems to get it just about right when he describes this latter, postmodern perspective as follows: "There still are boundaries, but they are blurred by all the crossings. We still know ourselves to be this or that, but the knowledge is uncertain, for we are also this *and* that" (1997, 90; emphasis in original). In embracing and almost celebrating paradox, here, Rabbi Soloveitchik seems to be abandoning the kind of certainty and knowingness I attributed earlier to his lonely man of faith. In reading and rereading this essay, we need to remind ourselves that we need not demand from Rabbi Soloveitchik, the author of the essay "Confrontation," the same degree of internal coherence and transparency that Rabbi Soloveitchik demands from the intellectual model he invents in his essay and labels as the lonely man of faith.

Rabbi Soloveitchik writes that the depth personality of the lonely man of faith never leaves its ontological seclusion and never becomes involved in a communal existence. If we take this literally, we must assume that Rabbi Soloveitchik himself is writing his essay and com-municating his ideas only at a "surface" level, as a kind of aside. Few who have studied the essay, though, would agree with this. And, as curious as we might be about the real Rabbi Soloveitchik, this curios-ity is beside the point. While it is true that we will never know how much of himself he revealed in this essay and how much of himself he kept concealed from us (this is one of the elements that makes great writing great), we do know, from our own points of view, how much the essay has affected us. We do know that Rabbi Soloveitchik's words have penetrated beyond our surface personalities to reach into our core selves and enlarge and transform them. Why else do we keep reading this forty-year-old essay? But, if his teaching can affect us like this, we also know it undercuts his description of the lonely man of faith because *our* depth personalities *have been* shaped and formed through *his* language.

Social life is about more than merely coordinating interests and exchanging services with one another. Dialogue is not just about trad-ing information in the marketplace of ideas, but dialogue allows us to relax our own conception of who it is that we really are. It allows us to see our own humanity reflected in the eyes of the other. In the end, the very real boundaries that protect and hold the lonely man of faith are self-imposed. It is precisely these boundaries that can, when we are ready, serve as the bridge to higher and deeper levels of consciousness. The move away from a comfortable traditionalism can be experienced as a kind revolution. It can be framed as a clean break from the past, an overcoming of lifeless boundaries. This same move, however, can also be experienced as part of the natural flow of life. One is carried from one way of making meaning to a new way. Growth is as much about continuity as it is about discontinuity. In reading Rabbi Soloveitchik's essay, "Confrontation," one is spectator to this kind of almost seam-less human development. More importantly, if one is able to turn off his or her own voice temporarily and learn to listen with respect, care, and patience, he or she can allow oneself to experience and undergo this same kind of development in response to Rabbi Soloveitchik's words. It is through the flow of dialogue that we can catch a fleeting glimpse of our "pluralistic universe" and begin to sense a true feel-ing of at-home-ness. As William James noted in the conclusion to his Hibbert Lectures delivered at Manchester College at the beginning of the last century, "In a word, the believer is continuous to his own consciousness, at any rate, with a wider self from which saving experi-ences flow in" (1909, 307). It is in lingering in the space of dialogue that we can overcome our "desire to fetishize the unity of the self" and replace it with a "love that melts bad boundaries to produce desirable change" (Reeve 2005, 34).

SOME GUIDELINES FOR CONDUCTING ETHICAL DIALOGUES

We live in lonely fear, huddled up, singly, against the protective walls we have erected. History teaches that this is not always an unreasonable way to live. There is evil in this world, and we must protect ourselves from it sensibly. We do this not only for ourselves but also for our children. Not everyone out there is our friend. There are real enemies in this world.

What is unreasonable is to attach certainty to our fears and to assume that this is always the only or best way to live. We hold onto our truth as if it is the whole truth, and we believe in the whole truth as if it is a thing we can possess. But, truth is a process. We are always at the border of a better world, even as we sometimes discover ourselves irrationally strengthening the boundaries that constrain us rather than tearing them down. We often forget that it is we who have built these self-imposed protections because they have so often served us well in the past. Ethical dialogue is not a cure-all. But, ethical dialogue is a way of living our lives more provisionally, more experimentally, and more fully alive to our real options. There is a risk in opening oneself up to the other, but there is a much greater risk in permanently sealing oneself inside impermeable boundaries.

Just as there need be specific preconditions for engaging in interfaith dialogue, there must also be preconditions for any kind of ethical dialogue. In the context of Jewish-Christian dialogue, Rabbi Soloveitchik stipulated four such preconditions: (1) it must be acknowledged that the Jewish people is "an independent faith community" and its worth is to be "viewed against its own meta-historical backdrop without relating to the framework of another"; (2) Jewish survival is non-negotiable; (3) "non-interference is a sine qua non for good will and mutual respect"; (4) each community has a "right to live, create and worship God in its own way, in freedom and dignity."

These preconditions can be generalized and made appropriate for any kind of dialogue, whether conducted between faith communities, nations, communities, or individuals. Here are my guidelines:

1. Each party's survival is guaranteed by the other party.
2. Each party to an ethical dialogue is independent and reserves his or her right to self-determination.

3. Each party pledges mutual respect and mutual recognition of the other party's integrity and dignity.
4. Each party pledges to express itself honestly and freely and to allow for the other party to express itself honestly and freely.
5. Each party reserves the right to exit the dialogue but also recognizes the possibility of interdependency.

It must be emphasized, however, that these guidelines are merely useful to jump-start a dialogue and may themselves become the subject of dialogue. We must never forget that the boundaries we self-impose can never possess anything more than a temporary degree of usefulness. While it is easy to forget, they are not fixed principles, but useful tools. In time, participants may discover more nuanced ways to reason and think together. They may expand or shorten this list, depending on the particular context in which the dialogue takes place and the particular purposes of the dialogue. As dialogues intensify, meaning evolves and is deepened, and preexisting structures may be overcome. To insist with certainty on a set of inviolable principles limits the real possibilities for dialogue and violates its inherent logic.

CONCLUSION

Stephen Mitchell notes that there are "certain forms of knowing, coercive forms, which strive to fix the fluidity and multiplicity of the other into a predictable pattern . . . It has strong appeal. It seems to be security-enhancing. But it is coercive and illusory" (2002, 45). This is exactly the kind of knowing that we must avoid in the context of ethical dialogue. We must avoid the temptation to put ourselves and others into a kind of lockbox from which it is impossible to escape.

John Dewey, the American philosopher, once wrote as follows about great art:

> A work of art elicits and accentuates this quality of being a whole and of belonging to the larger, all-inclusive, whole which is the universe in which we live. This fact, I think, is the explanation of that feeling of exquisite intelligibility and clarity we have in the presence of an object that is experienced with esthetic intensity. It explains also the religious feeling that accompanies intense esthetic perception, We are, as it were, introduced into a world beyond this world which is nevertheless the deeper reality of the world in which we live in our ordinary experience. We are carried out beyond ourselves to find ourselves. I can see no psychological ground for such properties of an experience save that,

somehow, the work of art operates to deepen and to raise to great
clarity, that sense of an enveloping undefined whole that accompanies
ourselves . . . [We] are citizens of this vast world beyond ourselves, and
any intense realization of its presence with and in us brings a peculiarly
satisfying sense of unity in itself and with ourselves. (as quoted in Jackson 1998, 61)

In reading Rabbi Soloveitchik's essay "Confrontation," I perceive it as
a work of art in Dewey's sense. I am introduced into a "world beyond
this world which is nevertheless the deeper reality of the world in
which we live." All ethical dialogues that work well are like this. Rabbi
Soloveitchik reveals, at best, a deep hesitancy about art and its worth.
In yet one more of his many paradoxes, however, Rabbi Soloveitchik
has created his own work of art. We do an injustice to ourselves and
to him if we do not let it speak to us anew each time we read it. In the
end, it is precisely *confrontation* with the other that liberates us from
the very boundaries that we choose to live within, from inside our
own depth personalities. It is through widening the circles of ethical
dialogues that our own loneliness is finally diminished and that we will
begin to perceive ourselves as part of something much bigger than
individual and isolated selves.

Ethical dialogues thus generate a unique view of spirituality. The
next section of this book explores several different aspects of this
emerging conception of spirituality.

PART II

SPIRITUALITY AND DIALOGUE IN THE CONTEMPORARY WORLD

CHAPTER 4

---—◦✦◦—---

INTELLIGENT SPIRITUALITY
IN BUSINESS*

In the Jewish tradition, there is a famous talmudic parable that describes an ancient debate: the rabbis are arguing, as is their usual practice, over a practical point of law. Rabbi Eliezer uses every conceivable argument to convince his colleagues that his opinion is the correct one. Although by reputation Rabbi Eliezer is considered one of the foremost experts in the particular area of law under debate, on this day, he fails to convince the majority in the conclave that he is right. Having failed in logically arguing his case before his peers, Rabbi Eliezer performs miracle after miracle, including uprooting a tree and causing the walls of the study house to lean in.

His colleagues were impressed with the miracles, but not overwhelmed. Rabbi Yehoshua, sensing Rabbi Eliezer's direct connection to God, even if he did not find his legal arguments convincing, turns to God and rhetorically asks, "If talmudic sages argue with one another about the halakhah [law], what affair is it of Yours?" Realizing that his mysterious and symbolic miracles were convincing to no one when it came to actually deciding the law, Rabbi Eliezer ups the ante and plainly states, "If the halakhah is in accordance with me, let it be proved from heaven." In fact, a heavenly voice directly intervenes. "Why are you disputing with Rabbi Eliezer, for the halakhah is in accordance with him everywhere?" (Baba Metzia 59b).

An overly pious reader might wish the story had ended here. One might think that from a religious perspective, there's not much left to say. God has spoken; the decision should be to follow the conclusion of Rabbi Eliezer. Isn't that what God wants? This, however, is not

*An earlier version of this chapter was published in *Research in Ethical Issues in Organizations* 5 2004): 63–94.

how the talmudic parable ends. In response to the heavenly voice, Rabbi Yehoshua thunders back, "It (the law) is not in heaven."

A postscript to the story adds that when God saw Rabbi Yehoshua get up and quote the written Torah against his own view, God smiled and said, "My sons have defeated me, my sons have defeated me." This is a remarkable and closely studied story in the Jewish tradition even today. Its theme is a perennial concern to every religious community. It contains many lessons to the astute and careful reader. I want to suggest, here, that it is this story, and other similar talmudic narratives that contain the seeds for the emergence of a new kind of religious sensibility. It is a deeply grounded, emotionally inspiring spirituality that is human-centered, pragmatic, and intelligent. As Rabbi Yehoshua tersely puts it, "It is not in heaven." The developing religious sensibility foreshadowed in this story, and explored in the remainder of this chapter, begins in contemplating and imagining the far-reaching implications of this new and revolutionary insight.

I call this new self-conscious religious attitude "intelligent spirituality." While the name is new, the idea itself has a well-respected pedigree in both Jewish and non-Jewish traditions. In the Jewish tradition, the contemporary Rabbi, Irving "Yitz" Greenberg, is the most prominent spokesperson. Outside the Jewish tradition, it is the American philosopher, educator, and activist John Dewey, who, more than anyone else, defined the parameters of intelligent spirituality, demonstrated its usefulness in the modern world, and, perhaps most importantly, exemplified it as a living option in his daily activities.

For those interested in the contemporary "spirituality movement"—advocates, critics, or spectators—and especially how it affects today's business organizations, the idea of intelligent spirituality provides a useful set of precise criteria to evaluate some of the many changes that are occurring in corporate America and are defended under the banner of spirituality in business. Can one distinguish, for example, between legitimate and illegitimate spirituality? Are some forms of spirituality more useful than others? To what extent can spirituality play a positive role in contemporary business? Is spirituality necessarily related to coerciveness and intolerance in business?

To define and explain intelligent spirituality, I will borrow from and build on one of John Dewey's most famous books on religion, a slim but influential work titled *A Common Faith*, published in 1934. The book was written when Dewey was seventy-four years old, and it is safe to say that it is a product of his mature philosophy and understanding (Rockefeller 1991). The book illustrates Dewey's inspired philosophical theory of pragmatism and shows how it offers a unique and important perspective on religious experience and spirituality. It is an especially useful perspective in understanding how spirituality can begin to play an important role in the contemporary world. He wrote, "Any activity pursued in behalf of an ideal end against obstacles and in spite of threats of personal loss because of conviction of its general and enduring value is religious in quality. Many a person, inquirer, artist, philanthropist, citizen, men and women in the humblest walks of life, have achieved, without presumption and without display, such unification of themselves and of their relations to the conditions of existence. It remains to extend their spirit and inspiration to even wider numbers" (27). Accordingly, intelligent spirituality is human-centered. Its point is not necessarily to participate in God's inevitable unfolding over time (as others have defined spirituality), but rather it is a process that, by design, culminates in a change in character and in the achievement and satisfaction of an ever growing set of human needs. Further, it is not just any set of human needs, but those needs that are understood at both an intellectual and an emotional level to further the growth and flourishing of the human community. At one point, Dewey states, the authentically religious is always "morality touched by emotion" (22). These spiritual activities help to unify the self and to integrate the self into society and the whole of reality.

Intelligent spirituality is not other-worldly (there is no other world that humans can access according to the pragmatists); rather, intelligent spirituality inheres even in the most frequent of activities, eating, drinking, making love, making friends, talking, and working, as long as these activities are deliberately and thoughtfully chosen as the means to achieve human values of enduring quality. This is not to say that one cannot distinguish between degrees of spirituality. Certainly devoting oneself to finding a cure for cancer is potentially more spiritual than pursuing a hobby of collecting beer cans from around the world, but the difference is one of degrees, not a difference in kind. There is no gap, as is often thought, between different kinds of spiritual activities. It is not the case, for example, from this perspective that prayer or meditation is sacred and work is profane. Work can be as sacred as prayer, just as prayer can be as profane as work. To summarize, pragmatism and its view of religious experience deliver a one-world theory.

TEN COMPLEMENTARY ELEMENTS
OF INTELLIGENT SPIRITUALITY:
ASSUMPTIONS AND PROPOSITIONS

To best understand what intelligent spirituality means to its contemporary practitioners, it is helpful to carefully dissect the above definition. In what follows, I will tease out ten complementary elements that together constitute this emerging concept, with special emphasis on those aspects that are especially important in today's pluralistic business environment. For clarity, I divide the ten elements into three assumptions and seven propositions.

Three Assumptions

Intelligent spirituality is human-centered and not other-worldly. As a practical matter, these observations stem from an important and crucial distinction between intelligent spirituality as it is being discussed here and other more common definitions of spirituality. *Intelligent spirituality, as a living possibility, assumes one can meaningfully distinguish between spiritual and religious experiences, on the one hand (I use these two terms, as Dewey does, interchangeably), and the supernatural and religion, on the other.* This primary assumption forms the basis for much of what follows. Most of Dewey's book *A Common Faith*, for example, addresses the possibility of just such a distinction and forcefully concludes (if somewhat apologetically) of the need to separate spirituality completely from the realm of the supernatural as it impinges on human affairs. In Dewey's framework, spirituality is a term of art that describes purposely human action in relation to the community and the natural environment. It does not describe a separate and transcendent realm of reality to which man can attach himself; spirituality is both *in* the world and *of* the world. Dewey's position assumes religious experience/ spirituality can be detached or unplugged from traditional religious assumptions in a meaningful and powerful way. He concludes the first chapter of his book in unequivocal terms. Starkly stated, "The opposition between religious values as I conceive them and religions is not to be bridged" (28).

The assumption that it makes sense to distinguish between religious experience, as perceived and felt from a human perspective, and the supernatural realm is a theme more recently explored in the work of Rabbi Irving Greenberg. Greenberg, whose work represents a theological response to the horrors of the Holocaust, echoes Dewey's religious humanism when he states, "It is too late for an all powerful Messiah to come . . . Bringing the Messiah is dependent on human intelligence, passion, and courage to help overcome the obstacles to perfection . . . The Kingdom of God can only be created if we bring people together and spread knowledge" (Greenberg 1998, 310). While Dewey would have distanced himself from the goal of "perfection," it is fair to characterize Greenberg's thought as an attempt to naturalize religious thought in the Deweyan tradition. Michael Oppenheim further elaborates on Greenberg's views:

> He [Greenberg] suggests that there have been three stages in the unveiling/development of the notions of redemption and covenant within Judaism. In the biblical period God was regarded as the sole redeemer and the covenant was a contract between unequals. God was the adult, the actor in history, and the Jewish people, his children remained loyal to the covenant primarily by being obedient. This biblical paradigm ended with the destruction of the two temples. In response to this catastrophe, the Rabbis rethought some of the basic concepts of Judaism. They recognized that God no longer directly intervened in history, which left that stage open to human initiative and responsibility. The covenant form was reconfigured to reflect a more equal partnership . . . In turn, the Holocaust demarcates the end of the rabbinic paradigm and the beginning of a new stage. It demonstrated that God is more hidden/limited than the Rabbis had believed. History and the movement toward redemption is now given over to human effort to an even greater extent. (2000, 192)

Greenberg puts the point boldly as follows: "God now acts primarily, at least on the visible level, through human activity—as is appropriate in a partnership whose human participant is growing up" (1998, 38).

This aspect of intelligent spirituality diverges sharply from some contemporary and well-respected definitions of spirituality. For example, Judi Neal, a highly articulate spokesperson for the burgeoning spirituality at work movement defines spirituality as follows:

> We are more than our bodies, more than our minds, more than our feelings. *We are part of a larger consciousness*, which some of us may call God. We are here to learn as much as we can so that we can evolve into a higher level of consciousness. When that happens, *we will see that we are not separate from anything and we will merge with all consciousness*. Like a drop of water that joins the ocean, we are aware of our individual selves, but we also become aware of our connection to the greater Self.

> In the process of our evolution, *we are helping the Greater Self—the essence of all that is—to discover, unfold, and celebrate itself.* This is our work. (2000, 1316; emphases added)

From the perspective adopted here, it is not at all clear that if it is "fated" that we are to merge eventually with the "all consciousness" as is implied here, and if it is already known that the Greater Self is engaged in a process of discovering, uncovering, and celebrating itself, why in the world does the Greater Self need any contribution at all on our part? According to the above, it is not a question of "if" all this will happen; rather, it is merely a question of "when" it will happen. Dewey is not afraid of the idea that spirituality can be thought of as an "expanding consciousness." I think he would have embraced this concept, but he is concerned, as will be argued later in the chapter, that the kind of supernaturalism—implied by phrases like the "all consciousness" and the "Greater Self"—can lead to a passivity and withdrawal from the world, even if that is certainly not its immediate or obvious intention.

At first blush perhaps, Dewey's insistence on rejecting the supernatural seems rather extreme; nevertheless, even traditional religionists like Rabbi Joseph Soloveitchik, the leader of modern orthodoxy in America for much of the twentieth century, on occasion have noted the need to emphasize man's independence from God. For example, perhaps echoing Rabbi Yehoshua's famous insight, he wrote, "that it is within man's power to renew himself, to be reborn and to redirect the course of his life. In this task, man must rely upon himself; no one can help him. He is his own creator and innovator. He is his own redeemer; he is his own messiah who has come to redeem himself from the darkness of his exile to the light of his personal redemption" (as translated by Peli 1980, 198). There certainly exist differences between Dewey's consistent and uncompromising rejection of the supernatural and Rabbi Soloveitchik's occasional embrace of human independence, but there is a common direction to the flow of their thoughts here. Both writers are engaged in a process of exploring the concept of human dignity and its potential importance to an authentically religious worldview (see also Soloveithcik 1965).

To the extent that one can distinguish between religious/spiritual experience and the supernatural, one can no longer rely on miraculous help from the transcendent sphere to help one solve her problems and improve her situation, nor can one seek out a meaningful life in response to a perceived supernatural framework. To return to the introductory parable, "it is not in heaven." Intelligent spirituality does not jettison the notion of meaning and purpose as human goals; rather, it seeks to clarify what meaning and purpose are from a purely human perspective. If meaning is to be found, it is not in mirroring a transcendent reality or striving after shadowy copies of preexisting, but other-worldly, ideals. If meaning exists, it is a product of human making. Or, stated more formally, *intelligent spirituality assumes meaning is potentially intrinsic to human activities.*

The philosopher Irving Singer carefully discusses this second element in his thought-provoking book *The Creation of Value* (1992). In extending the pragmatist tradition, he writes,

> Instead of seeking meaning of life as if it were something preexisting, we must study the natural history of mental acts and bodily responses that enable organisms such as ours to fabricate meaning for themselves. We speak of "finding" a life that is meaningful, but meaning is something we create. Whether or not we believe there is a prior system of intentions built into reality, we need to ask questions of a different sort: How do we actually create meaning? What is the phenomenology of a meaningful life? What will give meaning to my life? Is life worthwhile? (43)

It is true as traditional religionists and some critics of pragmatism have always known that humans are not free to unboundedly pursue hedonistic and individualistic pleasures. In intelligent spirituality there is "a note of submission" (Dewey, *A Common Faith*, 16). But such submission is voluntary in nature, it is not something imposed from outside. Dewey clarifies, "Conviction in the moral sense signifies being conquered, vanquished, in our active nature by an ideal end; it signifies acknowledgment of its rightful claim over our desires and purposes." It is the humanly envisioned ideal, grounded in experience and nature, which finally captures our imaginations and emotions. It is in actualizing an imagined better future—growth—in which meaning is born and responsibility is assumed. According to Irving Greenberg, "to reduce evil and suffering . . . bringing out to the fullest the individuality, the equality, and the value of every human being" represents the religious in the highest sense (1988, 322).

This means that intelligent spirituality is less likely to succumb to the disarming allures of utopianism. It is clearly recognized that if an imagined future is merely a daydream or an unattainable figment of imagination, it serves no positive purpose. In fact, utopianism may lead to an unhealthy and dangerous passivity and acceptance of the status quo. If an imagined future is not realistic and concrete in its details, it is automatically disqualified as an "ideal end." From a pragmatic point of view, an end with no feasible means of attainment is literally fantasy. Now fantasy may potentially serve a positive function, but one must never lose sight of the fact that it remains fantasy until one can imagine practical aims of attainment.

A third necessary assumption of intelligent spirituality states that *human progress is possible (certainly not necessary) but solely contingent on intelligent choice.* This is an idea that, while perhaps still out of vogue, is certainly making a comeback in some circles. The theologian Irving Greenberg might label this assumption as a "voluntary covenant," a strikingly bold phrase that combines a rich and suggestive biblical idea with an uncompromising humanism (1998, 55).

Consider one of the most outstanding business books in recent years, *Good Work: When Excellence and Ethics Meet,* inspired by the pragmatist tradition (2001). The book is authored by Howard Gardner, an internationally renowned cognitive psychologist (best known for his theory of multiple intelligences and his work on creativity and leadership); Mihaly Csikszentmihalyi (pronounced CHICK-sent-me-high), a social psychologist (best known for his work on flow); and William Damon, a developmental psychologist who has long worked on moral and social issues. Listen carefully to how these well-respected thinkers talk about the power of conscious choice: "But neither our genes nor the informational codes of our culture alone are responsible for how the future will unfold. The crucial final component in the causal chain is the code of consciousness—the use we choose to make of the instructions handed down by biology and culture. *The deterministic forces of the past are modified, rejected, or improved upon by ideas and ideals invented by individuals, and then shared by communities.* Hence, our vision of the future shapes what happens" (2001, 51; emphasis added).

The authors further explain that in the past it might have made sense from an evolutionary perspective to accept a kind of fatalistic philosophy where human choice is irrelevant. In an environment where human control is negligible, it might make sense to submit one's self to supposed supernatural forces. Certainly it provides a convenient excuse after the fact. "Whether we look to the stars for advice, believe that ultimately the will of the gods will prevail, or trust in the inevitable unfolding of the materialist dialectic, we then face a restricted range of necessary decisions for which we feel answerable" (2001, 51).

Fatalism is expressed in today's culture in a variety of ways. Belief in the invisible hand of the free market as a panacea for all our ills, trust in a ubiquitous Gaia, false Messiahs, New Age assertions of extra-terrestrial beings, or the fundamentalist belief that God will reward people for terror and the murder of innocents in an Eden-like future, are all manifestations of a helpless and hopeless philosophy of life. The point is, though, that in a technologically advanced interconnected world like the one we now inhabit, such a philosophy is self-fulfilling. According to Gardner, Csikszentmihalyi, and Damon, "Our hope clearly lies in our best individual and collective efforts, imperfect as these might be" (2001, 52).

What makes these remarks especially interesting is how matter-of-factly these authors insert normative prescriptions in a book that is advertised as essentially empirical in nature, marking a sharp departure from the typical positivism that dominated most academic thinking (especially in the social sciences) in the last century. I point this out not as a criticism, just the opposite. In my terms, these authors are outstanding advocates for, and contemporary examples of, intelligent spirituality in action.

An emphasis on intelligent choice is hardly unique to these authors. Other exemplars include the organizational theorists James March, Joseph Badaracco, Robert Quinn, James Collins, and Jerry Porras; the philosophers Michael Walzer, Charles Taylor, and Jeffrey Stout; the sociologists Amitai Etzioni and Philip Selznick, and many others. Despite many differences in both substance and method among these writers, what they all share in common is the fundamental belief that history *can and should* be shaped by conscious human choice in pursuit of enlarging and enhancing the human community. Such choice is neither arbitrary nor ad hoc; rather, it is guided by deeply felt concern and the careful weighing of experimental knowledge of how the world really works. "The art which our times needs in order to create a new type of individuality is the art which, being sensitive to the technology and science that are the moving forces of our time, will envisage the expansive, the social, culture which they are made to serve" (Dewey 1999, 49).

Erich Fromm, yet another psychologist, has summarized well the importance of intelligent choice, especially in the context of the problem of spirituality in business. He wrote,

> The nineteenth century said "God is dead; the twentieth century could say 'Man is dead.' Means have been transformed into ends, the production and consumption of things has become the aim of life, to which living is subordinated. We produce things that act like men and men that act like things. Man has transformed himself into a

thing and worships the products of his own hands; he is alienated from himself and has regressed to idolatry, even though he uses God's name. Emerson already saw that "things are in the saddle and ride mankind." Today many of us see it. The achievement of well-being is possible only under one condition: if we put man back into the saddle. (1981, 15)

To conclude this section, a number of explicit and implicit propositions, relevant to the top of sprituality in business, emerge, given the definition of intelligent spirituality and these three basic assumptions:

1. Intelligent spirituality requires a distinction between spiritual/religious experiences, on the one hand, and the supernatural and religion, on the other.
2. Meaning is intrinsic to human activities.
3. Progress is contingent on intelligent choice.

Seven Propositions of Intelligent Spirituality

The remainder of this chapter is devoted to a discussion of these propositions, as summarized below:

1. Intelligent spirituality occurs in time and is not a thing of space.
2. Intelligent spirituality requires deep change.
3. Intelligent spirituality can be a quality of any activity.
4. Intelligent spirituality is social.
5. Intelligent spirituality embraces both the method and findings of science.
6. Intelligent spirituality is a balance.
7. Intelligent spirituality is instrumental.

Exploring the Propositions of Intelligent Spirituality

Intelligent Spirituality Occurs in Time and Is Not a Thing of Space
It is probably true that most mature traditions have recognized some version of this first proposition as a central component to its vision of authentic spirituality. It is hardly unique to the pragmatist perspective of John Dewey and his followers, but it is still worth mentioning at the outset, if for no other reason than to demonstrate the time-honored roots of intelligent spirituality.

In Judaism, for example, this idea is underscored by the fact that the first time the term *kadosh* (holiness—a word that some have argued is the best Jewish equivalent to spirituality) appears in the

Bible is in describing a day, a period of time, rather than a thing. Neither the heaven nor the earth is described in the Bible as possessing holiness, as one might expect. Rather, it is in describing the Sabbath that the term first appears. "And God blessed the seventh day and made it holy" is how this idea is first couched in Genesis. Rabbi Abraham Joshua Heschel, one of the most important interpreters of Judaism in the twentieth century, believed that "Judaism is a *religion of time* aiming at the *sanctification of time* (1951, 8; emphases in the original).

As much as most of us give lip service to this proposition, it is difficult to absorb as a matter of practice and habit. It is easy to succumb to things on an emotional level even if we know intellectually that it is the meaning of things that really matter. All of this is not meant to disparage the tangible aspects of life. Things matter, too. But, they must always be viewed with proper perspective.

I was recently reminded of this when new friends invited my wife and me to a small party in their house. I had never been in the house before, nor had I even seen it from the outside, although I had heard it was beautiful. As we drove down their street, I gasped at the sheer size of the structure. It was literally twice the size of the other houses in the neighborhood. As we entered the house and took the "tour," I was amazed at the artwork, furniture, big-screen televisions, computers, and appliances. The host warmly explained how it was a "smart" house, wired with the most advanced technology to anticipate the family's needs in advance. As the party continued, I began to feel jealous. "This is great! I knew I should have become a high-priced lawyer like my mother wanted instead of a professor," I thought to myself. It wasn't until later in the evening that the host quietly confessed to us that he really thought of the house more like a museum than a home. His sad comment was probably due to the fact that both of his teenage children have recently moved out of the house to attend high school in another city at their own requests. It was only when he described his house as a museum that I was able to remind myself how difficult it is in the face of truly grand objects to live this first proposition; spirituality occurs in time, it is not a thing of space. It is not the house that should elicit our jealousy.

If anything is truly admirable about a house like this, it would be the planning—done in love and anticipation, the enjoyment of building the structure, and the meaning and texture of the living that takes place within its walls. None of this, of course, would be obvious to the casual visitor. If this is a beautiful house, which it very well might be, it is because it encourages a certain quality of life, not because of its size, contents, and cost.

Heschel spoke eloquently about the need to refocus our lives with the aim of more spiritual experiences. As he put it,

> Indeed, we know what to do with space but do not know what to do about time, except to make it subservient to space. Most of us seem to labor for the sake of things of space. As a result we suffer from a deeply rooted dread of time and stand aghast when compelled to look into its face . . . Shrinking, therefore, from facing time, we escape for shelter to things of space. The intentions we are unable to carry out we deposit in space; possessions become the symbols of our repressions, jubilees of frustrations. But things of space are not fireproof; they only add fuel to the flames. It is impossible for man to shirk the problem of time. The more we think the more we realize: we can not conquer time through space. We can only master time in time. (1951, 5–6)

Rabbi Abraham Joshua Heschel, writing in the early 1950s, anticipated a fast-growing twenty-first-century concern. He perceived more than many of his contemporaries at the time of the need to return to tradition—not to wax nostalgic—but to rediscover a spirituality relevant for the modern world. While many Jewish communities were frantically raising funds to build beautiful new synagogues, Heschel was sensing a lack of an authentic spirituality. Certainly it would be unfair to characterize Heschel's thought as pragmatic in nature. Nevertheless, his deep-thinking and passionate writing provide an important point of departure to contemplate the potential meaning of spirituality in our times. His poetic insights capture the essence of this first proposition. As he summarized, "We must not forget that it is not a thing that lends significance to a moment; it is the moment that lends significance to things" (1951, xx).

Talking about and trying to understand this proposition is one thing. But, how do we come to embody spirituality in time on a daily basis? It is to this question that we turn next.

Intelligent Spirituality Requires Deep Change

Quinn, Spreitzer, and Brown (hereafter "QSB") suggest the reason organizational change efforts often fail is because the underlying human system is not altered through such traditional change strategies that emphasize logic, power, and what they call normative reeducation. Real change occurs only when the people in the organization change. It requires painful adjustment and real sacrifice to enact change in a positive way. "In adaptive change, people must step outside known patterns of behavior—they must surrender their present selves and put themselves in jeopardy by becoming part of an emergent system. This process usually requires the surrender of personal control, the toleration of uncertainty, and the development of a new culture at the collective level and a new self at the individual level. In adaptive change, traditional change strategies are not likely to be effective" (2000, 147). Further, the authors believe that the only way to change others is to first change oneself. In this, they are not calling for a superficial change only at the level of observed behavior, but rather a fundamental and long-lasting change of character traits. This is what they call "deep change" and it is what links this discussion directly to "intelligent spirituality."

It is no accident that QSB claim that their initial insights came from a comprehensive examination of the lives of three of the greatest and most important spiritual leaders of all time: Jesus, Ghandi, and Martin Luther King Jr. It is their thesis that each of these leaders brought about great societal change because they first changed themselves. They did not view change in short-term strategic terms, but rather understood their projects as potentially global and far-reaching in nature. Deep change is not about meeting Wall Street's quarterly earnings expectations, but it is about changing the rules of the way the game is now played.

Their theory suggests ten overarching principles, all of which are consistent with the pragmatic tradition and serve to illustrate more clearly the contours of intelligent spirituality in business. The principles of "deep change" are as follows:

1. Seeks to create an emergent system
2. Recognizes hypocrisy and patterns of self-deception
3. Personal change through value
4. Frees oneself from the system of external sanctions
5. Develops a vision for the common good
6. Takes action to the edge of chaos
7. Maintains reverence for the others involved in change
8. Inspires others to enact their best selves
9. Models counterintuitive, paradoxical behavior
10. Changes self and system

While a full discussion of these principles is merited, it is beyond the scope of this chapter. Nevertheless, a few observations are still worthwhile here. First, with regard to the first principle, "seek to create an emergent system," this idea and this language perhaps, at first, sound similar to Judi Neal's definition of spirituality examined above and rejected. Recall that she talks about merging with the all-consciousness and in helping the Greater Self to unfold. It is true that this, too, is a kind of emergent reality, but the difference is in her version this is the inevitable pattern of history. It's going to happen whether or not any one of us participate. The QSB perspective makes no such grand (and unprovable) claims. In fact, in the fourth principle (free oneself from external sanctions), QSB emphasize what I previously stated as one of the founding assumptions of intelligent spirituality: progress is contingent on human choice. As the authors remark with regard to the fourth principle, "In reading the organizational studies literature, one would think that human behavior is largely shaped by situational influences and resource dependencies. There is work, however, that suggests that individuals are free and can make strategic choices." I would include the book by Gardner, Csikszentmihalyi, and Damon, discussed above, as the most recent and important example of such work in the field of behavioral studies.

In addition, it is also worthwhile to point out the similarities between the kind of deep change called for by QSB and traditional religionists. Once again, I return to the work of Rabbi Joseph Soloveitchik. In his book, *On Repentance*, he emphasizes that authentic repentance in the Jewish tradition is only achieved when the repentant goes through a complete metamorphosis. Basing his opinion on earlier authorities like Maimonides, he goes so far as to say that this requires one to become a new person, in some cases even taking on a new name.

In the business world, such change is rare, but possible. Joseph Jaworski's inspirational memoir, *Synchronicity: The Inner Path of Leadership* (1996) traces his own spiritual growth and what he dubs his "fundamental shift of mind" (9). This shift of mind is best illustrated in his recommendations to Royal Dutch Shell, which came about as a result of the global scenario project that he started in January of 1990. With prophetic accuracy, among his tentative conclusions, he noted, "the global scenarios for the next thirty years should principally revolve around the issue of the relationships between the rich and poor countries of the world" (1996, 152). He continued,

> We saw the world at an important turning point—what might be termed a "hinge of history." The liberalization might continue to spread into a world of rapid and unsettling change, with vast new competitive markets opening up in the developing countries. We saw this as "Scenario A," which we ultimately called "New Frontiers." On the other hand,

liberalization might be resisted and restricted, resulting in a world of divisions and barriers—a world deeply divided with huge disparities in wealth, with widespread poverty, urban crime, and disregard for the environment that inevitably accompanies desperation and hopelessness. This we dubbed "Scenario B," later called "Barricades." (1996, 156)

What is particularly interesting about Jaworski's work for Shell was his decision not only to describe these two potential scenarios but also to unabashedly call for Shell to help bring about the "New Frontiers" version rather than passively react to which ever future "happens" to occur. "There are also changes in ourselves in relation to the world in which we live that are much more inclusive and deep seated," wrote John Dewey in *A Common Faith* (1934, 11). Jawaroski's memoir documents one example of Dewey's insight. That his spiritual journey culminated in his work as a planner for an oil company suggests the next proposition.

Intelligent Spirituality Can Be a Quality of Any Activity.
In the United States, business success has often been the direct result of a stark either-or choice. There are two worlds: the world of business and the world of religion. If you want to make it in the real world, you better get practical and choose wisely.

The very first talking movie was produced by the four Warner brothers in 1927, the year Babe Ruth hit sixty home runs. The movie was called *The Jazz Singer* and starred Al Jolson as the son of an orthodox Jewish *chazan* (cantor) living on the lower east side of Manhattan. In the movie, the *chazan*, now on his deathbed, realizes that he will not be able to lead the Kol Nidre services, the most important religious service of the year for Jews. At the movie's climax, the old *chazan* still harbors some faith that his son, who is scheduled for his first Broadway performance that very night, will forgo his big break and continue with the long-standing family tradition of leading the services on Yom Kippur, the holiest day in the Jewish calendar.

Al Jolson's jazz singer, like all religious Americans of the twentieth century trying to make it here, faces a clear and unambiguous choice. His director and beautiful female costar in the Broadway play are pulling him one way; his old father and loving mother are pulling him the other way.

Business historians surmise that it was the Warner Brother Studios that first adopted the new technology of talking movies precisely because they were among the least established studios. The more entrenched studios were happy with the silent movies and the money they were earning from them and simply did not want to rock the boat. Perhaps there is another reason, though. Did the Warner brothers, Harry, Abe, Jack, and Sam, the ambitious and hungry sons of the orthodox immigrant, shoe repairman, Benjamin Warner, identify with the jazz singer's dilemma?

To a certain extent, the jazz singer's either-or dilemma is still our dilemma eighty years later. Nevertheless, a new chapter in the story is beginning to emerge. Today in business, a new perspective is being tested. Instead of looking at our lives as an either-or proposition, a new perspective of both-and is beginning to look possible. This perspective is at the heart of what I am calling intelligent spirituality.

I think it is much easier to understand what I'm talking about if I begin with a story from the world of politics first. Suppose you're sitting down for *Shabbat* (Sabbath) dinner after one of the most difficult weeks of your life. You are enjoying good food, good company, and a needed mental recess. As you begin to sing *Shabbat Zemirot* (traditional Sabbath songs), the door bell rings. It is a top aide of the vice president of the United States. He has sent one of those block-long limousines to pick you up. The vice president needs to speak with you immediately with regard to an urgent matter that will have profound effects for the entire country and world. What do you do?

Well, if you're Senator Joseph Lieberman, you tell the aide that you are enjoying your meal with your family and while you do understand the urgency of the call, you will walk to the vice president's mansion as soon as you are finished with your dinner.

It was this story and many others like it that motivated me to begin studying the issue of the relationship between business and religion more carefully. Thanks to a sizeable grant from Yeshiva University and special encouragement from former Dean Harold Nierenberg and Vice President Morton Lowengrub, I have now begun a project interviewing Jewish business people.

Let me share briefly with you some of their stories.

There is little or no difficulty in finding business men and women who continue to speak forcefully for the old and still dominant either-or perspective:

There was Josh, the highly successful 45-year-old business consultant, who runs a forty-person consulting firm in the suburbs of New York City. Josh describes himself as a traditional Jew. He often attends synagogue on Saturdays and he sends his children to a Jewish day school. When I asked him about the relationship between religion and work, he made it very clear that these are separate activities. He could not think of a single example where religion or spirituality played a role in a business decision. As Josh was thinking about this, he also noted that of his forty employees, not a single one was Jewish.

Then there was George, the treasurer of a major financial institution head quartered in New England. George was also quite articulate and adamant about the need to separate business and religion. He noted that while many evangelical Christians meet during lunch to engage in Bible study, it is not a practice that he would like to encourage. As our discussion continued, George did admit that, all things being equal, he probably would hire a Jewish employee over a non-Jewish one.

Deeply traditional Jews, I discovered, also embrace the either-or perspective. Baruch is an orthodox Jew. He studies the Talmud on a daily basis and regularly attends prayer services. He is a 1995 graduate of a top ten graduate business school and he now works as a computer analyst. Baruch, a few months ago, turned down a job at a computer company that self-consciously tries to bring religious values into the workplace. He declined the job because he felt the atmosphere was not very professional. In Baruch's view, as long as the organization he works for accommodates his religious requirements, especially Sabbath observance, he is satisfied.

Herbert, a retired lawyer from Texas, was less certain about the need for keeping religion out of the workplace. As our conversation warmed up, he told me stories about how he would purposely use Yiddish words in court before the non-Jewish judge or before a very Texas-like jury. In Herbert's view, his "Yiddishisms" and Jewish manner demonstrated a humanity and hominess that was disarming and ingratiating in a completely non-Jewish environment. He told me had he been practicing in New York City he probably would not have "played the Jewish card," as he put it.

There are other Jewish business people, however, who embrace and promote a very different philosophy. If we call the either-or perspective the two-world theory, we can call the newly emerging view the one-world theory, or returning to the language of this chapter, intelligent spirituality. According to this second theory, although it may seem as though we live in different worlds, it is important to minimize this psychological bouncing back and forth. There is a search for a more integrated life, a life of wholeness and integrity. One of the best ways to accomplish all of this is to openly talk about spirituality in business.

Consider 28-year-old Jeff, a graduate of one the best colleges in the country. Jeff has turned down numerous job offers in order to start his own karate school. Jeff, himself a black belt, openly acknowledges his desire to view his curriculum in spiritual terms. He is also extremely concerned about treating his employees fairly and honestly. Jeff and his teachers meet at least once a week to discuss the progress of each of their students. When Jeff talks about progress, he is not only talking about karate moves, but also the behavior and attitudes of his students. While Jeff struggles to meet his payroll and pay his rent expense, he maintains a calm and calming presence. Jeff's goal is to be an example for his students of a person whose external behavior and inner thoughts are always in harmony.

Bill attended one of the best law schools in the country. He practiced law on Wall Street for a few years and then set about on his life's journey. Bill, like black belt Jeff, views spirituality as a kind of connectedness and wholeness. During our interview, Bill, who sells coffee beans throughout New England, demonstrated the viability of the one world theory. He seamlessly discussed issues of finance and issues of fairness. He connected his highest aspirations to his most mundane business activities, fixing the coffee roaster. Bill is no pie in the sky idealist, but neither is he a through and through materialist. He sees a positive connection between spirituality and sound business performance. In his view, you can have your cake and eat it, too. Bill told me he pays above market prices for the raw coffee beans because of an epiphany he had at Yom Kippur services the previous year. "How can I beat my breast and ask for forgiveness, if my suppliers, from whom I earn a generous living, can not afford life's basic necessities?" Bill recognizes that he is engaged in a new kind of experiment. His smile and generous character suggested to me, at least, that so far, the experiment has been successful.

What is the lesson in all of this? It's like Bob Dylan says, "The Times, they are a changin'".

Rabbi Saul J. Berman, a contemporary rabbi and founder of Edah, tells the story of a young, religious lawyer who has taken a job with a prestigious law firm. He finds himself working eighty-hour weeks. While he enjoys the challenges and new responsibilities in his blossoming career, he is experiencing difficulties. The young man goes to his rabbi with whom he enjoys a special relationship. "There's something missing in my life, and I can't quite figure out what . . . I'm not married yet, so that's missing, but there's something else missing . . . I mean, like, you know, I used to have more inside me and . . ." (Berman 1999, 8).

The rabbi listens carefully to the young professional and his former student. The rabbi notes that what is missing is the kind of spiritual life his student enjoyed while he was studying in his Yeshiva. The rabbi recommends to the student that he begin a study program of one hour a day. The rabbi assures his former student that it doesn't matter whether or not the study session takes place at 6:00 in the morning or at 12:00 midnight. He can do it over the phone or even make use of the Internet. The essential thing is that the study session is fixed. The rabbi suggests that lawyer should learn at least one page of Talmud per day.

What is most interesting about this response is what it leaves out. The Rabbi correctly notes a kind of spiritual loss on the part of his former student. In his remedy, however, the Rabbi surrenders eighty hours a week to the "realities" of organizational life. It never even dawns on the Rabbi to suggest to the budding lawyer to find meaning inside the law firm, or to find a law firm where such a suggestion might be taken seriously by existing partners.

The eighty hours a week devoted to work and spent at the law office have nothing whatsoever to do with the one hour per day devoted to Talmudic studies, just as the Talmudic studies are completely divorced from the mundane and practical concerns of everyday life. It is as if the rabbi is telling his former student to cut himself in two. The rabbi, far from being the traditionalist he claims to be, is offering a kind of hyper-modern solution. According to Rabbi Berman this is not the Torah way: "The Torah has a different model, one that spiritualizes work. Does the Torah say to the farmer to work from morning to night, and, when he comes home, to sit and read a *parsha* [section] from the Torah? No. The Torah tells the farmer how to do farm work in a way that puts spirituality at the core of his activities. It breaks down his productive efforts into the smallest possible units and fills them with Torah values" (Berman 1999, 8–9). Most of us are not farmers today. But, the lesson that spirituality needs to be built into productivity is still a contemporary message. As Rabbi Abraham Heschel once put it, "it is a mistake to regard the sacred and the profane as absolute contrasts. For some parts of reality to be endowed with sanctity, all of reality must be a reflection of sanctity. Reality embraces the actually sacred and the potentially sacred." "A Chassidic rebbe said that wisdom and wealth were both virtues but wisdom the greater. Someone asked him, 'Why, then, do the wise wait upon the rich, and not the rich upon the wise?' The rebbe answered, 'Because the wise, being wise, appreciate the value of wealth, but the wealthy, being only wealthy, don't understand the value of wisdom'" (Halberstam 1997, 9). Perhaps this sociological reality is beginning to change.

Intelligent Spirituality Is Social
All of the people I have relied on above to define and explain intelligent spirituality have been uncompromising on this point. They are

all sensitive to the limitations of classical eighteenth and nineteenth century liberal definitions of man as isolated and atomistic. From the perspective adopted here, it is impossible to envision the individual as completely separate from the community in which he was born and now lives. Individuals are embedded in community, even as one continues to aggressively assert the hard-won human rights owed to each and every individual.

Advocates of intelligent spirituality have no difficulty in understanding the behavior of the Tom Hanks' character in the movie, *Castaway*. In the film, Hanks portrays a hard-driving, time-obsessed executive of the FedEx Corporation who is the sole survivor of a plane crash in the South Pacific. He is washed up on an island and survives for years by exploiting the contents of a few FedEx packages (containing ice skates, video tapes, etc.) that also happen to survive the plane wreckage, and by relearning many of life's most basic lessons: how to make a fire, how to open a coconut, and how to build some simple structures. Most importantly for my purposes, the Hanks character invents an imaginary companion out of a volleyball he finds in one of the packages. After painting a primitive looking face on the ball with his own blood, Hanks begins talking to his new "friend" as if it was real. In a sense, of course, it is. By sharing his thoughts and pretending he has a companion—in the movie, he calls the ball "Wilson"—the castaway is able to maintain a sense of himself, a sense of reality. It is understandable, from the perspective adopted here, that when "Wilson" drowns, the Hanks character breaks down and cries for his lost friend. For the Hanks character, as for all of us viewing the film, it is not difficult to imagine an imaginary companion saving one's life, but it is a life without any kind of companion that is truly unimaginable.

Intelligent spirituality is social. This is an important point to emphasize, as a separate proposition, because almost every spiritually based community has a tendency to draw sharp boundaries between insiders (true believers) and outsiders. There is often a temptation to stand apart and attempt to withdraw from the world, as if this were a possibility (if you're not in the world, where are you?). This is true both for traditional religious communities and for their new-age cousins. Dewey, in one of his most penetrating insights, would attribute this tendency to bifurcate our world to the continued insistence on supernaturalism. "It is of the nature of a religion based on the supernatural to draw a line between the religious and the secular and profane, even whet it asserts the rightful authority of the Church and its religion to dominate these other interests. The conception that 'religious' signifies a certain attitude and outlook, independent of the supernatural, necessitates no such division" (1934, 66). He asserts that this "doubleness of mind" will continue until "religious meanings and values are definitely integrated into normal social relations" (1934, 70). In other words, the two-world hypothesis follows directly from a belief in supernaturalism.

In traditional communities, spirituality (and final redemption) is usually reserved for communal-insiders exclusively. Unfortunately, this assumption often prevents spiritual-seekers to ever find what it is they are really looking for. For those readers interested in a personal account of intelligent spirituality, and the difficulties of finding it in traditional religious communities because of the false walls it often erects, I highly recommend, *Dance of a Fallen Monk: The Twists and Turns of a Spiritual Life* (Reading, MA: Addison-Wesley, 1995) by George Fowler. Fowler summarizes his life experiences, which include, among other things, a seventeen year stint as a Trappist monk who adhered to an oath of silence. In the end, he concludes, "I spent years grubbing around the globe for something to eat, having all the while a pocket filled with priceless stones. Or, in the metaphor of Meister Eckhart in the fourteenth-century west and of Buddhists before him in the East, I was a man riding an ox looking for an ox to ride on" (1995, xv).

Majia Holmer Nadesan, in a critical article of the spirituality in business movement, provides a number of examples of how a new-age philosophy can lead to a rejection of community in favor of a focus on self: "The discourse on corporate spiritualism often prescribes specific strategies for 'turning within' to discover and nurture the authentic self and for fostering expressivity. These strategies include 'meditation, self-hypnosis, induced altered states of consciousness, and guided visualization' where the intent is to change or control thought processes" (1999, 9). In the study, Nadesan identifies a sales and marketing executive who closes his door for twenty minutes every day to meditate, another manager who attends monthly Zen retreats, and a third who stares at himself in the mirror for ten minutes each morning before shaving. Each of these business executives believes that work issues are best resolved, not through actively changing the environment in which business is conducted, but by withdrawal and a turning a way from work. My point is not that there is anything wrong with strategies that include prayer and meditation, but they are dangerous to the extent that such strategies lead to a purposeful neglect of intelligent human choice and action.

Advocates for new-age spirituality often give up on the rest of us and seek solace isolated from a larger community, sometimes even taking up a confrontational stance to the wider world. For example, Judi Neal cites numerous examples of spiritual-seekers leaving business or limiting their involvement in business and seeking spirituality elsewhere. Her interviewees, like the office-worker, Maureen, often tend to conflate spirituality with a pulling away from reality. As Neal describes her, Maureen believes that everything she prays for, she receives. She told Neal during the interview, "Prayer. I pray all day long. I talk to God constantly. I know all my prayers by heart." Neal summarizes her findings. "It is probably easier to practice the concept of work as service to the Divine in situations where we are volunteering or where we are not being paid much for our work and are doing it for the simple love of doing it . . . Spiritual masters advise students to stop being outwardly focused and attached to the material world and to start focusing more inwardly on their experience of soul and their connection to the Divine" (2000, 1322). While Neal does later admit, "not everyone who sees work as a spiritual path has to give up a higher paying job to find their calling," it certainly seems that withdrawal is her first-best solution.

A major distinction between intelligent spirituality and both traditional and new age versions is the latter's seeming insistence on "a non-attachment to outcomes . . . in the process of performing actions." To the extent that intelligent spirituality is social in nature, this nonattachment to outcomes is ruled out completely. Neal concludes her paper by noting that about 25% of the population have strong spiritual values. By contrast, I would suggest that intelligent spirituality being both of the world and in the world is not a matter of the luck of the genetic lottery nor is it attached to place. In fact, since it is solely a function of intelligent choice and action, it is potentially available to all.

To a large extent, the social character of an activity can itself serve as a criterion to evaluate its degree of spirituality. This suggests a number of specific implications for spirituality in business.

1. Intelligent spirituality cannot endorse one set of ethical rules for insiders and a separate set of rules for outsiders.
2. Profit maximization can not be the single criterion to evaluate corporate performance. One must always ask to what extent are corporate outputs satisfying legitimate human needs. Are corporate actions increasing or diminishing the breadth and depth of community?
3. Organizational culture is not just a tool to provide tangible outputs; organizational culture either enhances or detracts from intelligent

spirituality. Organizations must become more self-conscious about the fact they are locations where human beings interpret life's meanings. Dewey was as emphatic on this point as on any other. "Industry must itself become a primary educative and cultural force for those engaged in it" (Dewey 1999, 65). This is because "Social institutions, the trend of occupations, the pattern of social arrangements, are the finally controlling influences in shaping minds" (Dewey 1999, 62).

To conclude and summarize this section, I quote from the very last paragraph of Dewey's *A Common Faith*, which captures the essence of the social nature of intelligent spirituality.

> The ideal ends to which we attach our faith are not shadowy and wavering. They assume concrete form in our understanding of our relations to one another and the values contained in these relations. We who now live are parts of a humanity that extends into the remote past, a humanity that has interacted with nature. The things in civilization we most prize are not of ourselves. They exist by grace of the doings and sufferings of the continuous human community in which we are a link. Ours is the responsibility of conserving, transmitting, rectifying and expanding the heritage of values we have received so that those who come after us may receive it more solid and secure, more widely accessible and more generously shared than we have received it. Here are all the elements for a religious faith that shall not be confined to sect, class, or race. Such a faith has always been implicitly the common faith of mankind. It remains to make it explicit and militant.

For Dewey's aspirations to become a reality, the next proposition is a necessary condition.

Intelligent Spirituality Embraces Both the Method and Findings of Science

I have come to believe that the project of integrating science and religion is not a path that is likely to lead to any kind of satisfaction. The very idea that there is a need to integrate science and religion is based on faulty logic. The basic problem as I now see it is that the project of integrating science and religion begins by assuming what it hopes to disprove.

Let me explain. Those interested in demonstrating the fit between science and religion assume at the outset that science and religion are making competing claims, that somehow science and religion are in the same business (i.e., creating useful knowledge). For example, science demonstrates the high likelihood of evolution as an explanation of man's origins, while traditional religion attempts to defend a premodern conception of creation and the creative process. Integrationists attempt to resolve a seeming contradiction here. Perhaps the scientist and the religionist can reach some tolerable compromise and a temporary detente is found. In time, though, science becomes more aggressive. Another round of compromise is called for. Again, a creative solution is found, and the never-ending process continues.

The problem here is not in finding ever more ingenious solutions to show the consistency between religion and the new emerging conclusions of science, as the integrationists have claimed. Rather, the problem is the continued insistence that somehow there can be a rivalry between science and religion (to begin with) and therefore a perceived need to integrate. Once one has allowed for this possibility, the hope of integration is itself illogical. In other words, the attempt to integrate science and religion is the problem, not the solution.

An example of what I'm talking about can be found in Ken Wilber's book, *The Marriage of Sense and Soul: Integrating Science and Religion* (1998). The purpose of Wilber's book, as the name explicitly states, is to uncover a more advanced way of thinking about the relationship between science and religion, one that takes both the claims of science and the authentic claims of religion seriously.

Wilber's solution in this book and elsewhere is to distinguish among the three levels of being: body, mind, and spirit. There is no inherent contradiction between science and religion because science and religion are different ways of knowing different aspects of reality. According to Wilber, the eye of flesh (empiricism) represents an attempt to know the body, the eye of mind (rationalism) is concerned exclusively with knowing the mind, and the eye of contemplation (mysticism or religion) provides knowledge about spirit. As Wilber explains it, empirical science "can tell us much about the sensory domain and little about the mental domain, but virtually nothing about the contemplative domain. And no "new paradigm" is going to alter that in any way. Chaos theories, complexity theories, systems theories, quantum theories—none of them requires scientists to take up contemplation or meditation in order to understand those "new paradigms," and thus none of them gives any direct spiritual knowledge at all. They are just more mental ideas hooked to sensory perceptions; they are not transmental contemplation disclosing the Divine" (1998, 36). In the end, it turns out Wilber's need to "marry" sense and soul is a mere artifact of his arbitrary division of reality into three hermetically sealed regions. Contrary to Wilber, the best way then to "integrate" science and religion is to simply refuse to divide reality in the first place in this way. The assumption of intelligent spirituality is that there really is only world after all, and there can be no "spiritual knowledge" divorced from it. Spirit is not a separate realm of being; rather, spirituality is grounded in empirical reality as we know it through science.

Scientific discovery itself can be a spiritual activity to the extent that it is undertaken with the goal of improving human society in a reasonable and practical way. It is not a thing apart as Wilber and all integrationists assume from the get go. Alan Briskin is surely right when he poetically concludes his important book, *The Stirring of Soul in the Workplace*, "When spirit loses its depth and substance, when it does not descend into the realities of the body, then we can say it has no soul. And when the body no longer seeks the struggle brought about by vision and ideals, then we might also say that the coarseness of life is no longer leavened by spirit, breathed fresh each day into a living soul" (1998, 20).

This proposition entails a number of implications for the spirituality at work movement. Most importantly, I want to suggest that spirituality must be grounded in empirical reality. An executive who makes her decisions based on astrological calculations, for example, is violating the basic tenets of intelligent spirituality. This is why Ian Mitroff and Elizabeth Denton's recent book, *A Spiritual Audit of Corporate America*, (1999) represents an important first step forward in our understanding of this topic. Based on extensive interviews, the authors draw a number of important tentative conclusions with regard to spirituality at work. Their study was exploratory in nature. Rather than quibble with their methodology and conclusions, it should be viewed as an invitation to more rigorous and precise empirical testing in this area.

Intelligent Spirituality Is a Balance

Ideals, as a product of human imagination, are experimental and uncertain. That ideals are a product of human imagination is explicitly implied in each of the three assumptions outlined at the beginning of this chapter. In turn, this observation must necessarily imply the fragile and imperfect nature of ideals. We can never know, with perfect certainty, what it is that we really want, nor how to obtain it. We choose ideals to promote human interests, but the ideals themselves are subject to revision and improvement. The balance referred to in this proposition is not a balance between the spiritual and the material, but rather, it is a balance in forming and choosing ideals.

Advocates of the "rational model" of decision making, by contrast, believe there is a once and for all formula for arriving at the best decision in any given situation. Economists, like all rationalists, think that decision making is always about arriving at the most efficient choice in a given decision context. That single choice that maximizes expected future utility is the one and only best choice. Decision makers are asked to identify all possible actions, to link those actions with outcomes, and to rank outcomes in terms of personal preference. The action that will most likely lead to the most preferred outcome is the rational choice. From the perspective of intelligent spirituality this can't be.

In a changing world, where our ideals evolve over time, where our knowledge of the future is imperfect, where our very identities are tied up in the communities in which we were born and now live, rational decision making often breaks down. Ironically, one might suggest that the attempt to apply the rules of rational decision everywhere is itself "irrational." There are many situations where there is no one right answer to a dilemma. Some decisions are so important that they not only reveal and test who we are, but they also shape our future character. The choice of which college to attend, whom to marry, what career to select, where to live, would all seem to fall into this category. The decision, in these kinds of right versus right cases, not only affects outcomes in the world, but the decision also turns back at us and affects our very personalities and character.

These kinds of decisions not only occur in our personal lives, but they occur at work as well. For example, the decision to fire a long-time employee will affect the future prospects of the employee but will affect the boss as well. A decision to market a controversial product will impact society, but will also reveal much about the decision maker and shape his future character.

John Dewey described these kinds of critical decisions as follows:

> Now every such choice sustains a double relation to the self. It reveals the existing self and it forms the future self. That which is chosen is that which is found congenial to the desires and habits of the self as it already exists. Deliberation has an important function in this process, because each different possibility as it is presented to the imagination appeals to a different element in the constitution of the self, thus giving all sides of character a chance to play their part in the final choice. The resulting choice also shapes the self, making it, in some degree a new self. This fact is especially marked at critical junctures. (Dewey and Tufts 1932, 317)

Joseph Badaracco, Jr. explicitly citing Dewey here, calls these "critical junctures" defining moments.

Of course, it is impossible to provide a fixed program for what to do in these situations, but Badaracco does successfully articulate a set of clear guidelines that serve to help decision makers who face defining moments. Although Badaracco himself does not use the term "spirituality," I believe his questions clarify the meaning of a spirituality that works in the real world. He suggests managers in facing tough ethical situations (like the prospect of a huge layoff) answer a set of questions as follows:

> How do my feelings and intuitions define, for me, the right-versus-right conflict?
> Which of the responsibilities and values in conflict have the deepest roots in my life and in my communities I care about?
> Looking to the future, what is my way?
> And how can expediency and shrewdness, along with imagination and boldness, move me toward the goals I care about most strongly? (Badaracco 1999, 82)

These questions suggest a number of characteristics associated with intelligent spirituality. As is implied in the first question, emotions count. In fact, this is where one starts. "How do my feeling define . . . the conflict?" While emotions count, however, they are never singly determinative. Decision makers must also consciously step back and ask themselves about the sources for these emotions. Where are the roots of my values? But, the grand principles associated with historical communities are not always binding. In defining moments, one must always ask, "What is my way?" Intelligent spirituality, unlike traditional religionists who try to deny this, recognizes that there is no way around this fundamental question. One can never remove the self from taking ultimate responsibility for a decision. One can invoke grand principles as a tool for framing a decision, but in the end the best that grand principles can do is to summarize the wisdom of the past. In a changing world, principles can never be authoritative in and of themselves. In the final analysis, there is no way to deny that an important decision is a reflection of "my way," of my ideals, my hopes, my aspirations, my identity. In short, intelligent spirituality is humanistic. Finally, Badaracco's last question reminds one that high aspirations alone are insufficient. Unless one has a realistic plan to implement one's choice, it really is no choice at all.

In business, Tom Chappel, of Tom's of Maine, has been quite articulate on the issue of intelligent spirituality. He writes:

> The Middle Way is not . . . a kind of compromise. It's a course that
> keeps in view competing aims: working efficiently versus taking time
> out for respect; making money versus being kind; having a kick-ass
> attitude versus having patience. The Middle Way is not "this way" or
> "that way," either-or; it's one way that integrates both. How is it that
> Buddha is serene yet mighty? How is it that Christ is meek yet majestic?
> It's because of how they did things—it's because of the practice of the
> Middle Way in their lives . . . Like a boatman navigating a swirling river,
> Tom's of Maine has to steer between analysis and intuition, between
> our goals of profit and social responsibility, between softball and hard-
> ball. (1993, 184–85)

Jeffrey Stout, a contemporary philosopher deeply influenced by the
pragmatist writings of John Dewey, provides a useful summary for this
discussion. The kind of balance called for here requires intelligence,
integrity, and human imagination. It is an attempt to harmoniously
weave together the strands of our cultural inheritance to produce
a usable cloth. Balance is not a bouncing back and forth from the
spiritual world to the physical world, nor is it even an integration of
these two separate worlds. Rather, "our task, like Thomas Aquinas's,
Thomas Jefferson's, or Martin Luther King's, is to take the many
parts of a complicated social and conceptual inheritance and stitch
them together into a pattern that meets the needs of the moment. It
has never been otherwise. The creative intellectual task of every generation, in other words, involves moral bricolage. It is no accident
that Aquinas, Jefferson, and King were as eclectic in using moral
languages—and no shame either" (1988, 292). The idea that intelligent spirituality must meet the "needs of the moment" leads to the
final proposition.

Intelligent Spirituality Is Instrumental
What this proposition says is that spirituality can be said to be intelligent, if and only if, it works. The idea of instrumentalism is an important idea at the heart of the philosophy of pragmatism. Dewey actually
preferred to call his philosophy instrumentalism rather than pragmatism. It is also one of the most misunderstood and unfairly maligned
concepts related to pragmatism.

In colloquial usage, the term pragmatism is often incorrectly used
in a pejorative sense. For example, an elected official who suddenly

abandons the ideology on which he based his campaign in order to promote his own political interests might be described as a pragmatist. An academic dean who lowers academic standards in order to attract more students to his school might justify his actions and attempt to end the conversation by noting, "I'm just being pragmatic." Or, a business manager in a company long known for treating its employees fairly might defend her decision to fire 1,000 employees by noting that under the circumstances it was the pragmatic action to take. To the extent that the elected official, the dean, and the business manager are abandoning long-held beliefs to promote their own individual short term interests, none of these decisive actions "work" in Deweyan instrumentalist terms. Ironically, in each of these three cases, Dewey would have strongly condemned the actions rather than applauded them. These actions "work" only if one is willing to abandon his or her ideals willy-nilly, something that Dewey himself would have abhorred. Pragmatism is often incorrectly contrasted with vision-based management. It is wrongly thought that a pragmatist would be willing to abandon the vision the moment it becomes inconvenient. Nothing could be farther from the authentic spirit of philosophical pragmatism.

If instrumentalism is not about abandoning one's aspirations, beliefs, and ideals for short term gains, what is really implied by the statement that intelligent spirituality works? Intelligent spirituality works only to the extent that it helps to improve character, "it forms the future self," both at the level of the individual and at the communal and organizational level. Rabbi Zusya, many years ago stated that in the world to come, God will not ask "Why were you not Moses, or Akiba, or Abraham?" But, he will be asked, "Why were you not Zusya?"

Returning to the above examples, an intelligently spiritual politician would be one that projects a clear and attainable vision to his fellow citizens, a vision informed by the needs of his society but encompassing enough to encourage growth, openness, and maturity. As Vaclav Havel, one of the most articulate spokesperson for the kind of spirituality advocated for in this chapter, has put it, "I am convinced that we will never build a democratic state based on rule of law if we do not at the same time build a state that is—regardless of how unscientific this may sound to the ears of a political scientist—humane, moral, intellectual and spiritual, and cultural. The best laws and the best-conceived democratic mechanisms will not in themselves guarantee legality or freedom or human right—anything, in short for which they were intended—if they are not underpinned by certain human and social values" (1992, 218).

A spiritual dean is driven by academic criteria. He is first and foremost an educator. Only to the extent that his philosophy is inspiring and practical to faculty and students in a fast changing technologically advanced world can it be said to be spiritual. His school is not about pouring information into students heads, but is about providing students with a rich environment conducive to learning.

Turning to the business manager, she is successful as a manager, only to the extent that her decision reveals, tests, and shapes her character and the character of the organization that employs her. The truly great managers recognize that spirituality occurs in time and is not limited to a specific location, it requires deep change, it can be a quality of any activity, it is social, it is grounded in the best that science has to offer, and it requires self-conscious choices to promote carefully chosen and balanced ideals. Finally, none of this matters unless intelligent spirituality works.

CONCLUSION: THE USE OF INTELLIGENT SPIRITUALITY IN BUSINESS

For those who continue to view the world in the dualistic terms of spirituality versus materialism, there are three possible coping strategies with regard to the problem of integrating religion and business; there are the dualists, the accommodationists, and the warriors. Robert Wuthnow, the well-regarded sociologist of religion, based on his extensive research, makes this point as follows: "The spiritual realm and the material realm can be compartmentalized, viewed as separate worlds, within virtually any of the major faith traditions. The two realms can be synthesized in such a way that little but harmony between them can be imagined. They can also be pitted against one another as combatants fundamentally opposed in how they envision the good life" (1996, 300-301). Wuthnow provides numerous examples to illustrate each of these coping strategies. Here are some of them.

There is the middle-aged executive who lives in New York City and attends a Presbyterian church. Wuthnow describes him as a dualist who compartmentalizes his life. "I don't think God will hold up a scale on judgment day and balance out everything you've done," he told the interviewer. He continued, by emphasizing how economics is probably of little or no concern to God. "If you believe in Jesus Christ, then everything will be all right" (1996, 301).

Then there is the fashion designer who Wuthnow sees as an accommodationist: "He's glad . . . that the assistant rector at his church is a woman. 'She's absolutely wonderful. A gorgeous, gorgeous woman in every possible way, which is a delight when she's up on the pulpit. At least it something to look at.' Not wanting to sound too lustful, he also explains how nice it is that his son can see from an early age that God is an equal opportunity employer . . . Church practice for him is much like his beliefs. Take it or leave it; live and let live" (313). Lastly, there are the warriors. Consider the interviewee who told Wuthnow, "I'm a Christian who also happens to sell Canon copiers" (316). Or the Catholic woman who describes the place where she works as "alien." She says, "all they do is conduct business and manufacture things" (319). In her case she tries to get into her coworkers lives and show them some kindness.

This chapter suggests that Wuthnow's categories are misleading. It suggests that the very notion of a "coping strategy" may be mistaken. One needs a coping strategy only if one assumes a two-world theory to begin with, as Wuthnow apparently does. Further, if there really did exist a spiritual world and a material world, it is doubtful that any humanly-conceived coping strategy would work to bridge these two unbridgeable worlds.

Interestingly, even in Wuthnow's own interviews, it is clear that almost every one of his interviewees recognized at least some of the assumptions of intelligent spirituality. In almost every answer, there are attempts to disentangle the natural world from the supernatural realm. And, there is a recognition that meaning, at least on occasion, can be found at work as a product of conscious human choice, and not something that must always be linked to a transcendent reality. It is probably true that few of those interviewed by Wuthnow would extend these insights as far as Dewey and other pragmatists have. Nevertheless, had Wuthnow been looking for it, he would have found, as I did in my research and interviews, numerous examples of intelligent spirituality at work. Dualists, accommodationists, and warriors are not the only groups who seek spirituality at work. Practitioners of intelligent spirituality also seek it; the important difference being that they not only seek spirituality *at* work, but they also seek spirituality *in* work.

There a number of reasons to be optimistic about intelligent spirituality in business. First, the pragmatic philosophy that undergirds it is consistent with the basic business values dominant in contemporary organizations. Most business managers are pragmatists, whether or not they have ever heard of John Dewey and his followers. Second, it doesn't ask individuals to divide themselves in to two, as more traditional notions of spirituality seem to entail. It insists on a one-world theory. Third, in abandoning the quest for certainty, it allows for a real pluralism, beyond mere toleration. Fourth, it encourages each and every one of us to utilize the best resources available for solving ethical dilemmas. The sole criterion here being, does it help? For some, this may mean using philosophical theories, for others, this will include borrowing from a rich and textured religious heritage. Finally, its precise definition of spirituality provides a framework for a critique of current business practices (especially those activities advertised as spiritual), and a model encouraging the growth of both the individual and the organization.

To conclude, intelligent spirituality is an attribute of human behavior. It includes any consciously chosen activities pursued in behalf of realistic goals—ideal ends—because of a deep conviction of their general and enduring value. To some this may be too little, to others this may be too much, but from a pragmatist perspective, the only place one can begin the quest for spirituality is where one is. As the ancient rabbis already knew almost two thousand years ago, "it's not in heaven."

CHAPTER 5

SPIRITUALITY IN (AND OUT) OF THE CLASSROOM*

If work does not gladden me, I need to consider laying it down. When I devote myself to something that does not flow from my identity, that is not integral to my nature, I am most likely deepening the world's hunger rather than helping to alleviate it.

—Parker J. Palmer, *The Courage to Teach*

The theological problems seek to be translated into human terms and the human problems seek their way into theology's domain.

—Franz Rosenzweig, as quoted in *Kabbalah & Eros*

This chapter is divided into two sections. In the first section, I discuss "what is spirituality?" In the second section, I examine some of the implications of my definition to the teaching of spirituality in an undergraduate business ethics course.

I. WHAT IS SPIRITUALITY?

This chapter is not an attempt to figure out what spirituality *really means,* nor is it an attempt to figure out the *ultimate nature* of ethics. I leave these questions to others. Rather, I am self-consciously building and rebuilding a map to help me navigate through life's obstacles, opportunities, joys, and horrors. The sole criterion I choose for the success or failure of this chapter is the pragmatic one of whether or not it works. Does the proposed map help us to live a deeper and more connected life? Or, to quote William James, "Her only test of probable truth is what works best in the way of leading us, what fits

*An earlier version of this chapter was published in the *Journal of Business Ethics* 73, no. 3 (2007): 287–99.

every part of life best and combines with the collectivity of experience's demands" (1991, 38).

This is where I find myself: in the here and now. I am part of something much greater than myself, but I sense my own uniqueness even
as I accept my own limitations. The point is to "receive willingly" and
to embrace this simplest and most basic of all truths.

To listen and to discover life's internal rhythms; to enrich my life
and to deepen it; to uncover my desires and to name them, to discover
new ones, and to fulfill and satisfy these desires in a way that is itself
desirable. In short, I aspire to persist, to enjoy, and to love.

To my mind, the word *spirituality* most usefully describes a quality
of everyday experience: an experience of growth and oneness or a feeling of being at home everywhere in this vast universe. Spirituality is
going home to a place that you've never been before. This experience
can be associated with many kinds of practical and prosaic aims, activities, and projects. It is this-worldly and not other-worldly.

Spirituality is deeply personal, but at its very best it must be shared
with an other or others. We can speak to one another about spirituality
(after the fact), but at a deeper level we participate, facing one another
with eyes wide open, in a shared experience (mutually acknowledged)
of growth and oneness. Perhaps this is what the mystics call holiness.[1]

Martin Buber once wrote that "the world is not understandable
but it is embraceable; through the embracing of one of its beings."
This is the kind of natural spirituality to which my map is pointing.

The Promise of Spirituality: Blending Integrity and Integration

For my purposes in this chapter, I define spirituality formally as the
planned experience (the inner feeling) of blending integrity and integration through (a) acceptance (of the past), (b) commitment (to the
future), (c) mindful action, and (d) continuous dialogue (both internal and external). This definition is a work in progress and offered
mainly as a point of departure rather than a final destination.

Integrity is about being one's self and living in this moment. It is
being authentic to one's past *and* being true to one's future. Integrity
just doesn't happen by chance. Integrity is the hard-won result of the
successful (or partially successful) search for meanings and purposes
in one's life.

Here's a simple truth about spirituality that has taken me a lifetime
to acknowledge: I am my body, nothing more and nothing less. Or, I
am a kind of organization evolving in space and through time. I have

a past, a present, and a future. My awareness of my own self looms huge, and so I must remind myself that it really is a tiny dot in a corner of a constantly expanding cosmos.

Integration means connectedness, being part of a whole. It means that I accept my own insufficiency. I need and desire you as you need and desire me. I am attracted to you even as I fear you and am repelled. To talk of myself as a single body, unattached and alone, as integrity demands, seems incoherent.

There is a wholeness to the world: each of the tiny pieces interlock like a gigantic puzzle and form a unity. But, integration is even more than this. Pushing this thought to its limit, there are no tiny "separate" pieces at all; reality is a single puzzle piece.

Spirituality occurs in those precious moments when we grasp hold of both integrity and integration simultaneously. Or, better yet, it occurs in those moments when integrity and integration grasp hold of us.

It is a heightened state of awareness and aliveness. And it is a deeper kind of consciousness that is both self-aware and nearly perfectly attuned to the environment at one and the same time.

Although my description is perhaps beginning to sound too esoteric to be of much use, hardheaded empirical psychologists are now attempting to identify and talk about it in terms similar to those I am using. Here is how one psychologist describes it:

> Such feelings—which include concentration, absorption, deep involvement, joy, a sense of accomplishment—are what people describe as the best moments in their lives. They can occur almost anywhere, at any time, provided one is using psychic energy in a harmonious pattern. It is typically present when one is singing or dancing, engaged in religious ritual or in sports, when one is engrossed in reading a good book or watching a great performance. It is what the lover feels talking to her beloved, the sculptor chiseling marble, the scientist engrossed in her experiment . . . One of the most often mentioned features of this experience is the sense of discovery, the excitement of finding out something new about oneself, or about the possibilities of interacting with the many opportunities for action that the environment offers. (Csikszentmihalyi 1993, 176–77)

Spirituality is a state of mind that can embrace one's own reality as part of infinitely larger reality. One's experience of time is altered. One's confidence is enlarged. One is doing and being done to at the same time. In moments of spirituality one's deepest desires are in the process of unfolding and being fulfilled.

How Is Spirituality Achieved?

What I have described so far is the promise of spirituality. But is it really doable? I believe it is, but it requires a set of practices that include (among others, I'm sure) acceptance, commitment, mindful actions, and dialogue. Here is what I mean by each of these.

Acceptance

I do not think it is an accident that in Judaism the most mystical and spiritual of its traditions is described as the Kabbalah, a word that is derived from the Hebrew word meaning to receive or to accept.

Without acceptance, there is no spirituality (i.e., there is no blending of integrity and integration). Acceptance is a way of being in the world. It is being reverent. We stop struggling against reality. It is seeing yourself as part of a whole and giving up the arrogant picture of yourself as standing outside of (or above) reality and judging or manipulating it.

Sometimes, I think that to the extent that one can achieve a genuine and complete acceptance, one has already accomplished all of the practices identified here with spirituality. I want to be very careful here because we often mistake acceptance for resignation and passivity. This is not at all what I mean by acceptance. In fact, resignation is the opposite of what I am talking about. Resignation implies a withdrawal or a moving-away. Acceptance has an active quality. It is a joining or a merging not by doing but by recognizing something that has always been there. It is a mind-shift.

The world is the way it is, and no judgment or cynicism on my part will change this. So often I discover myself getting angry at the world or attempting to flee from it in fear. But this is like banging your head against a wall or trying to hide in a wide-open field. The world is horrible and scary (at times), but compared to what?

No matter how hard we try or how much we wish, we can not transcend our own experiences. We are forever part of this good and evil (hospitable and inhospitable) world. One of the greatest temptations we face is magical thinking. This is the precise opposite of acceptance. I cannot change it simply because I do not like it or because I don't want it this way.

To grow, to develop, to expand; I must begin where I am with what I have. Everything else is an example of magical thinking. There is a famous biblical story of Jacob struggling with an angel in the dark of night. Interestingly, his victory is not in subduing the angel, but in achieving a stalemate. It is what it is. Acceptance is to choose to stop wrestling with angels.

Instead of carrying the world, let the world carry you. Acceptance is going with the flow. Last winter, I was sledding with my children and as I was racing down the hill out of control and full of fear. I suddenly remembered to surrender to what was happening. Relax and enjoy the ride. And I did. In the end, I think, this is really all I mean by acceptance. In some ways it is so simple and yet, at the same time, there is something seemingly hardwired in us that continues to resist no matter how hard we try or how much we know better. "It can't be," we reflexively think, and yet it is.

Commitment

To what am I committed? What are my goals and beliefs? Where are my loyalties? Where do I stand? There is no certainty with commitment, and this is disconcerting to us. Commitments are like anchors. They keep us steady in a storm, but they can be hoisted at will.

Sharon Daloz Parks describes commitment as follows:

> If thinking doesn't bring us to certainty, why think? The answer usually comes from the imperative of ongoing life. Certainty may be impossible, but we still make choices that have consequences for ourselves and those we love. Particularly in relation to important life choices, a person may begin to look for a place to stand, a way of dwelling viably in an uncertain world. He or she may begin to value those ways of composing truth and making moral choices that are more adequate than other options. This is a search for a place of commitment within relativism.
>
> The formation of commitment in a relativized world requires taking self-conscious responsibility for one's own thinking and knowing. Now one becomes conscious of joining other adults in discerning what is adequate, worthy, and valuable, while remaining aware of the finite nature of all judgments. (2000, 59)

To perceive one's self-chosen commitments is a mark of maturity. It means that you have come to understand the happenstance of your own birth and upbringing. You do not reject your past, but you stop worshiping it.

You begin to stand up for yourself and you begin to wonder how best to achieve your own desires and not someone else's. You question whether or not your own desires are truly desirable. In a world that often seems as if it is beyond repair, you ask, "How can I help?"

Commitment is fueled by desire, and this is really scary because so many of us have been taught and programmed that our desires are base and primitive. A spirituality that tries to deny our own desires or overcome them seems to me to be inhuman, and so bound to fail. In truth, I am more scared of selfless love than selfish love.

Commitment includes hope and promise. It is about the future and not about the past. It is the practice of spirituality on which integrity most depends. It literally holds us together over time.

Mindful Actions

> To finish the moment, to find the journey's end in every step of the road, to live the greatest number of good hours in wisdom.
>
> —Ralph Waldo Emerson, as quoted in Miller 2000, 44

Mindfulness is being immersed in the here and now, not for some other sake, but simply for the sake of this moment. Here is how a young man describes the act of rock climbing:

> The mystique of climbing is climbing: you get to the top of a rock glad it's over but really wish it could go on forever. The justification of climbing is climbing, like the justification of poetry is writing; you don't conquer anything except things in yourself . . . The act of writing justifies poetry. Climbing is the same: recognizing that you are a flow. The purpose of the flow is to keep on flowing, not looking for a peak or utopia but staying in the flow. It is not a moving up but a continuous flowing; you move up only to keep the flow going. There is no possible reason for climbing except the climbing itself; it is a self-communication. (as quoted in Csikszentmihalyi 1993, 180)

To me, what this climber is describing is mindfulness, and this is an essential component of spirituality. Mindful action knows what it is doing and why it is doing. To be mindful means to be fully present, curious, aware, and alive.

John Dewey, in his book *Art and Experience*, talks about the difference between recognizing and perceiving. This distinction is helpful in understanding the difference between mindlessness and mindfulness. Merely recognizing a person or a situation always stops short of what is potentially possible. "Bare recognition is satisfied when a proper tag or label is attached, 'proper' signifying one that serves a purpose outside the act of recognition—as a salesman identifies wares by a sample" (1934, 53). In recognition, there is an habitual kind of mindlessness.

Perceiving, on the other hand, is more active and participatory. Perceiving means we move beyond our memories and preconceived ideas. Perceiving is a going-out and a meeting of an other. It is both cognitive and emotional. In Dewey's words, "Perception is an act of the going-out of energy in order to receive, not a withholding of energy. To steep ourselves in a subject-matter we have first to plunge into it. When we are only passive to a scene, it overwhelms us and, for lack of answering activity, we do not perceive that which bears us down. We must summon energy and pitch it at a responsive key in order to *take* in" (1934, 53; emphasis in original). To perceive, in Dewey's sense, is to be mindful.

Mindful action is risky action because we open ourselves up to scrutiny, and scarier still, we open ourselves up to the possibility of profound change. In being mindful, we allow ourselves to evolve in response to what is out there.

Dialogue

> *The decisive theme in the romance of moral success is the idea of an ordeal of vulnerability to hurt by others and to transformation by your own deeds, an ordeal from which you emerge triumphant. It is a triumph of the ability to throw yourself into an uncontrolled world in a way that, instead of annihilating you, allows you to exist more freely: freer from the compulsions of your character and from the quest for an illusory preemptive security against everyone else; freer to experiment with forms of action, collaboration, and vision. You lose the world that you hoped vainly to control, the world in which you would be invulnerable to hurt, misfortune, and loss of identity, and you regain it as the world that the mind and the will can grasp because they have stopped trying to hold it still or to hold it away. The world you can make a home in is a world that you no longer hope to control from the distance of immunity, and the character you can accept as your own is a character that you can at least see as but a partial, provisional, and pliable, version of your own self. Renunciation and loss, risk and endurance, renewal and reconciliation; these are the ancient incidents in the search to make yourself into a person during the course of a life.*
>
> —R. M. Unger, *Passion: An Essay on Personality*

In dialogue, there is a flow of meaning among the participants. A dialogue is not the same thing as a discussion or a debate. In dialogue everyone is committed to making meaning together. Or, in William Isaacs's words, it is "a shared inquiry, a way of thinking and reflecting together" (1999, 9).

To participate in a dialogue requires one to listen to another, to respect one another, to suspend one's own beliefs and to let go of one's judgments, and to express one's unique voice. In dialogue, we move beyond toleration and argumentation into a place where we feel comfortable reflecting about our own thoughts and attachments. There is a mutual recognition that this not about you or me, but it is about us. Dialogue, at its best, is transformative. One leaves a dialogue different from the way one enters.

In dialogue, we are accountable to one another and we are responsible for one another. We shower attention on one another and thus fulfill one of life's greatest desires. In dialogue, we finally feel as if we are home (again).

Dialogue is not just about identifying a set of facts. Dialogue is about emotions. How do we feel about each other? In dialogue, I must be true to my anger, fear, joy, sadness, and love, just as I must respect the full spectrum of your emotions.

Dialogue is also about identity. The very point of dialogue might be thought of as trying to figure out what it means to be us. Dialogue, like all of the practices identified above, demands openness, honesty, and imagination. In a real dialogue, I might suddenly take your point of view and you can take mine because we both realize that our talk is not really about promoting our own views. As I begin to see things as you see them, my own view is altered.

Rabbi Nachman of Bratslav once said that "the whole world is a narrow bridge, and the most important thing is not to fear." This kind of a bridge is an apt metaphor for dialogue. There is a deep fear in joining together with others, and our dialogues should openly recognize this fact. But, I think, we should be even more afraid of standing alone, singly. Dialogue is the bridge that connects us, and this is exactly why it is so essential to spirituality and the blending of integrity and integration.

For the purposes of explication, I have presented acceptance, commitment, mindful actions, and dialogue as separate and distinct practices. But, of course, this is not quite right. Each of these practices is related to the others. Dialogue depends on acceptance. Mindful actions cannot really be separated from dialogue. Acceptance and dialogue are held together through commitment. And, so on and on.

Is This Really Spirituality?

My dictionary defines *spiritual* as "relating to or affecting the human spirit *as opposed* to material or physical things" (emphasis added). The definition of spirituality that I am offering is very different from this one. In fact, I might define spiritual as relating to or affecting the human spirit *as it connects to* material or physical things.

Throughout this chapter and the previous one, I have emphasized the this-worldly and human aspect of spirituality and have been silent about the supernatural and God. So, why bother to use the word spirituality at all? Why not just jettison spirituality all together in favor of different words like meaning or meaningfulness (Pava 1999)? Introducing spirituality into this kind of a conversation is confusing, at best, and misleading, at worst.

I believe the word spirituality is too important and valuable a tool to leave behind only for the traditionalists to use. It is a word that still evokes our deepest attachments, and it is a word that one approaches with the utmost respect and care. It is a word that summarizes and points to some of the highest achievements of men and women.

Perhaps it is true that modernity demands that we sacrifice this word. If so, I'm not convinced yet. Another word like *meaning* could probably do most of the work I am assigning to spirituality, but, at the end of the day, I think it is missing something important that the word spirituality still conveys.

I like the word spirituality because I believe it is provocative in the positive sense that it provokes us to think more deeply about our experiences of integrity and integration. After all is said and done, there is a mystery to the word spirituality that I would like to self-consciously preserve.

The word spirituality is also useful in that it links us to our history and our past. While I readily admit that I am reinterpreting spirituality, I also believe that there are important common features to the underlying experience I am trying to describe and the underlying experience of traditionalists who use this same word. In fact, I believe that my description captures, with its emphasis on integrity and integration, the most important, salient, real, and enduring features of this common experience.

It is also a word that can serve as a bridge between traditionalists and modernists. Imagine a dialogue where traditionalists and modernists come together to better understand each other. What better word to focus on than spirituality? Let us be clear at the outset that we are using the word in different ways, but let us also try to imagine how we might be able to make meaning with this word together.

There is no use in demanding that all of us continue to use the word spirituality when we are referring to the experience of accomplishing integrity and integration. Demanding something like this would be to turn spirituality into a kind of idol. And, neither traditionalists nor modernists would want this.

To conclude this first section, I return to the beginning. Does the proposed map help us live a deeper and more connected life? To me, the answer to this question is yes, so much so, that I aspire to share this map with my students in my undergraduate business ethics class. But, is this possible? And, is it a good idea? It is to these questions that we now turn.

II. TEACHING SPIRITUALITY
TO UNDERGRADUATES

The essence of hospitality is located not in a warm smile and a hearty handshake but in the ability to create a meaningful shared space in which our attentions and intentions are aligned.

— R. Kegan and L. L. Lahey, *How the Way We Talk Can Change the Way We Work*

It is one thing to create one's own map; it is quite another thing to invite others in to share the map, especially when they are from a different generation and background and may embrace a very different conception of religion. There are many good reasons why one might not want to introduce spirituality into an undergraduate business ethics course. Students, whether or not they are conventionally "orthodox," tend to enter college as traditionalists in the sense that their thinking tends to be authority-bound and dualistic. Further, there is a remarkable degree of "conformity to cultural norms and interests" (Parks 2000, 92; see also Kegan 1994). Their understanding of spirituality as being other-worldly and encompassing the supernatural is generally a well-entrenched idea.

To students, spirituality isn't so much about the *inner experience of blending integrity and integration* as it is about following directions and being a well-behaved member of a spiritual community or tribe. To the extent that these observations hold in practice, might not a definition of spirituality like the one described above create an even bigger rift between me and my students?

Joey's Dilemma and Mine

Consider the case of a former student of mine, Joey Levine (not his real name). Joey told me about the following incident as part of his final project for the business ethics course he completed with me a few years ago.

Joey, twenty years old, came into class and witnessed a student rummaging through some stuff on the teacher's desk. The teacher had come into class earlier, but had then ducked out to make a quick telephone call. At the time, Joey didn't think about what the student was up to. "I gave him a funny look and I smiled as I walked passed him." His curiosity, however, was piqued when he heard a group of students laughing t

ogether as the class started. Here is how Joey describes it:

> A few minutes later Professor Albert wandered into class and began his lesson in the usual manner. He gave a little background to the case that we were going to study and began putting some numbers on the board. All at once there was an uproar of laughter from the back of the room that trickled up to the front as more of the class discovered what was so comical. After the commotion died down, the guy next to me let me in on the joke. Before the class began, there was a group of people copying down what they thought was the midterm. It turned out that in reality it was that day's lesson.

As Joey experienced this incident, he didn't really think much of it. "Business as usual," I guess. A few days later, however, Joey got a message that the dean would like to speak to him as soon as possible. After a little investigation, Joey discovered that everyone in the class was being called in. "They were searching for the person who stole the midterm!"

While Joey really didn't know who had stolen the midterm, he did know at least one person who had *tried* to steal the midterm. He describes his dilemma as follows: "I had always thought of two precepts to be true. One was taught to me from my parents and teachers, that I always must be honest in my dealings. The other was learned on the proverbial playground. This was that I must never betray a friend, no matter what the cost." Although Joey did not initially divulge any information to the dean, he felt unsure about his decision and spoke with his rabbi about what he should do. The rabbi, as it happens, was in the midst of spearheading a campaign to reduce cheating on campus. He told Joey that he, Joey, had an unambiguous responsibility from a Jewish legal and ethical point of view to divulge any and all information that he had about the midterm to the dean.

> Was I going to rat on this guy I do not even know, and jeopardize his future by getting him kicked out of school? Or, was I going to tell the rabbi, who was almost salivating over the chance to offer his first sacrifice to his new cause?
>
> Faced with these two options, the obvious choice for me was to tell on the attempted cheater. I consider myself a religious Jew. Part of my religion is that I heed my opinions to those rabbinic authorities I deem fit. Thus, when presented with an unqualified rabbinic directive, I followed without looking back.

Joey believes that this was a defining moment for him. "To make this decision, I had to realize what kind of a person I was, and act on that definition."

All of this was Joey's dilemma. Now, here is mine: As Joey's teacher, is it fair for me to sit and judge him as falling short of *my* definition of spirituality? As I study his story carefully, I, to be honest, can't help but be disappointed in his decision to abdicate his own responsibility in all of this and to hand over the decision to his rabbi.

It certainly doesn't appear that Joey himself is committed to "rat on this guy," nor is Joey practicing reasonable choice and mindful action. Most disheartening of all, Joey fails to engage the rabbi in any kind of dialogue whatsoever. Joey never challenges or asks why the rabbi decides the way he does. He doesn't seem to think that the reasons for the rabbi's decision are even relevant to the case at hand. Joey's sole job seems to be to "heed my opinions to those of the rabbinic authorities."

As I attempt to accept Joey (and all of his classmates) and respect the integrity of his decision, I wonder about my own role as teacher here. I want to meet Joey where he is and provide him with good enough company for the right journey. I want to challenge him, but not confuse him. I want to engage him in dialogue and not shut him down. I want to be alongside of him even as I lead him out. This is a delicate balancing act.

Integrating organizational ethics and spirituality, as Joey's case illustrates well, is a difficult and perhaps risky enterprise. Sometimes, I feel like I'm throwing my students into the deep end of the pool without a life jacket. For this reason, I am often hesitant to even use the word spirituality with my students. But, the five practices of spirituality that

I have identified, I believe, constitute many of the key elements for good leadership in today's business world and are ignored at our own peril. (See especially Badaracco 2002; Heifetz 2001; Heifetz and Linsky 2002; and Gardner 2004 for some contemporary discussions on leadership consistent with the assumptions of this chapter.)

Learning business ethics requires not just an ability to learn a long list of dos and don'ts, but it also demands a change in consciousness (Buchholz and Rosenthal 2000). This is a tall order that many of us are just beginning to appreciate. After all, we are asking students to leave behind (sacrifice) a part of themselves in order to move ahead. From their point of view, it is difficult to imagine how they might engage spirituality in the way I am advocating *and* maintain the integrity they have already achieved *and* continue to be well-behaved members of the tribe.

I am not trying to argue students out of their position, but I am trying to provide them with a comfortable environment in which they can begin to critically evaluate their own beliefs and values. In my class, we use dialogue, drama, biblical and Talmudic sources, literature, movies, and many other tools to accomplish this.

I would like students to deepen their connection to their religious heritage, not by indoctrinating them, but by giving them tools to self-consciously choose how best to satisfy their own desires and needs. I want to foster their curiosity and not stifle it. I want students to feel uneasy with themselves, but not too uneasy.

I suppose the biggest challenge of all is to model the four practices each and every day in an open and transparent way (to the extent that this is possible). As I contemplate the meaning of this last sentence, I wonder about my own motives and intentions here. Why I am so hard on Joey? In fact, he is to be truly admired as one of the few students I have ever known who has mustered up the courage to whistle-blow (despite knowing the costs that are usually associated with it). Perhaps Joey's paper stimulates my own inner doubts about ethics and rabbinic authority and my own struggles with what it really means to live a life of integrity and integration in a world of uncertainty and danger? Is the fact that I am a rabbinical school dropout of any significance to this discussion? Perhaps his story is not subsumed by mine (as I think), but a direct and live challenge?

Guidelines for Teaching Business Ethics and Spirituality

This is a difficult chapter to write. In admitting my own doubts, I fear I appear soft and confused. I have left myself open to criticism and attack. This is an especially dangerous impression to leave to business students who are looking for the one right answer and feel they have little time for contemplation and wonder in the "real time" of business.

Despite the legitimate reservations I have noted here, after all is said and done, I continue to believe that it is important to link business ethics and spirituality in the undergraduate classroom because the five practices are integral to business ethics, understood in its broadest terms.

Here are some guidelines to help:

First, *be clear and precise about your teaching aims.* In my business ethics class, I have settled on the following goal. My explicit purpose in teaching business ethics is to help students become full partners in a dialogue centered on business ethics. It is not my direct intention to get students to be "more ethical" or "more spiritual." I have selected a more modest goal because it is concrete and can be measured and monitored (both formally and informally) over the course of the semester. It is an appropriate one for an academic setting where all of us come into the classroom with different aspirations and values. It emphasizes process over content, and it is a skill that will serve students well as they begin their professional lives. (See the appendix for an open letter to my students describing my teaching philosophy.)

Will this goal ultimately lead to more ethical decision making? To the extent that one believes, as I do, that ethical actions are—by definition—those actions that flow from legitimate ethical dialogues, the answer is yes.

Second, *use material that is meaningful and appropriate to students.* In my undergraduate business ethics class, for example, we spend a lot of time discussing the issue of cheating in school. I do this because it is my belief that it is more beneficial to talk about personally relevant issues like this than broader social issues that students are just beginning to contemplate. It certainly does not have to be either/or. In fact, it is often sensible to ask students to link up the issue of cheating in college with an ethics failures like Enron and Andersen (for further examples, see Pava 2005).

Third, *listen carefully to what students are actually saying—not what you think they are saying.* The harder we listen as teachers, the more we can learn from our students.

For example, as I continue to consider Joey's dilemma described above, I wonder if there isn't more happening here than meets the eye. For sure, Joey believes that he has ultimate responsibility to obey his rabbi. Nevertheless, even in Joey's case, there is a seeming double message that he is conveying. I note that Joey goes out of his way to mention the rabbi's self-interest in this situation. Remember, the rabbi was spearheading a campaign to wipe out cheating. Further, Joey certainly paints a less than ideal portrait of his rabbi as "salivating over the chance to offer his first sacrifice to his new cause." This is, at best, a strange and unusual way to describe a rabbi to whom one is pledging his full allegiance. And, finally, Joey notes that he obeys only those authorities "I deem fit." So, although there is a gap between my view and Joey's, perhaps it is not quite as large as I first imagined.

Fourth, *reduce the fear*—one's own and one's students'. Students come into class with a kind of swagger and a thin self-confidence that masquerades a deep fear of looking helpless and uncertain to their peers and teachers. Just like teachers. To overcome this fear we need to build classrooms that are transparent and safe sanctuaries, and we must remind students that we are all in this together.

Fifth, *work hard and take chances*. The only way to get students to open themselves up to the opportunities of change is to open ourselves up to these same opportunities. Be a role model. This means we must continually experiment with new ideas and projects. If it works, great, if not, move on.

Finally, for those of us trying to integrate spirituality into the curriculum, *don't turn spirituality into an idol.* Keep in mind that it is not the word spirituality (or any other word, for that matter) that is intrinsically valuable, but the underlying experience of blending integrity and integration (to which the word is merely a pointer). The word spirituality is simply a tool. To the extent that it gets us what we really want, let's use it. Otherwise, be creative and find a substitute.

CHAPTER 6

LISTENING TO THE ANXIOUS ATHEISTS

When we allow ourselves to be fear-ridden and permit it to dictate how we act, it is because we have lost faith in our fellow men—and that is the unforgivable sin against the spirit of democracy.

—John Dewey, as quoted by Steven C. Rockefeller

I believe, despite all, that the peoples in this hour can enter into dialogue, each of the partners. In a genuine dialogue each of the partners, even when he stands in opposition to the other, heeds, affirms, and confirms his opponent as an existing other. Only so can conflict certainly not be eliminated from the world, but be humanly arbitrated and led towards its overcoming.

—Martin Buber, "Genuine Dialogue and the Possibilities of Peace"

The democratic procedure has the power to generate legitimacy precisely because it both includes all participants and has a deliberative character; for the justified presumption of rational outcomes in the long run can solely be based on this.

—Jurgen Habermas, "Religion in the Public Sphere"

In the past five years, several important books promoting atheism have been published. In this chapter, I examine four of these in detail. The purpose here is neither to refute the authors nor to critique their arguments, but to enter into a dialogue. The four books I discuss include:

The End of Faith: Religion, Terror, and the Future of Religion by Sam Harris (2004),
Breaking the Spell: Religion as a Natural Phenomenon by Daniel C. Dennett (2006),
The God Delusion by Richard Dawkins (2006), and
God Is Not Great: How Religion Poisons Everything by Christopher Hitchens (2007).

There is so much to learn from and agree with in the four books under review in this chapter. There is no doubt that "there is clearly a *sacred* dimension to our existence, and coming to terms with it could well be the highest purpose of human life" (Harris 2004, 15; emphasis added), as Sam Harris, perhaps paradoxically to some readers, writes in the opening pages of the first of these four books on radical atheism (each of the three books that follows cites Harris with nothing but approval). Similarly, we can all agree with Richard Dawkins when he admits openly, quite surprisingly perhaps, "that science's entitlement to advise us on moral values in problems is problematic, to say the least" (2006, 57). One can surely agree with Chistopher Hitchens who says that "the ignorant psychopath or brute who mistreats his children must be punished but can be understood. Those who claim a heavenly warrant for the cruelty have been tainted by evil, and also constitute far more of a danger" (2007, 52). Finally, Daniel Dennett, in echoing the philosophy of the great twentieth-century Jewish theologian Martin Buber, is correct in writing that "we can do no better than to sit down and reason together, a political process of mutual persuasion and education that we can try to conduct in good faith" (2006, 14).

I respect each of these thinkers. And their beliefs, reasoning, and theories, even if not wholly new or entirely convincing, deserve to be heard, understood, and debated. And, presumably, at the end of the day, *this is all they are really asking of us*. I agree with these authors that we are in the midst of a global crisis and that religion, and religious leaders and authorities, need to be held to high standards of accountability, perhaps higher standards than ever before in history, since the stakes—our very existence—are so high.

But, if Dennett and the others are correct, as I believe they are, and the best that we can hope for is "to sit down and reason together," one *is* entitled to wonder out loud about all of the strident rhetoric, exaggerations, bullying, and lack of respect and sympathy toward those with whom you disagree. Would not the purposes of the "new atheists" be better served through the (admittedly declining) traditions of civil discourse and dialogue rather than through hyperbolic rhetoric and threats? One wonders whether or not these authors have committed Dewey's "unforgivable sin against the spirit of democracy?" Have these anxious atheists, fearful, and understandably so in the age of anti-intellectualism, global terrorism, and other heinous sins, committed in the name of institutional religion, simply, "lost faith in our fellow men"?

To whom do these new in-your-face atheists imagine they are writing? Surely, they can't be writing to the "fundamentalist religious extremists" who, by their definition, are unwilling to reason and whose beliefs are invariant to states of the world, in any event. Nor, do I believe, that they are writing to fellow hardcore atheists who already agree with their conclusions. Rather Harris, Dennett, Dawkins, and Hitchens are writing to the rest of us, those of us who consider ourselves religious, but not fanatically so, those who continue to profess a belief in God, or merely "a belief in the belief" in God, as Dennett wryly puts it. They are writing specifically to those who continue to harbor the faith that there is a good chance that religion and religious resources will help us to resolve our seemingly intractable problems rather than exacerbate them.

We moderates, of course, might be wrong about religion. It may very well be the case that religious beliefs are nothing more than incredibly clever and pernicious "memes" that have attached themselves to us and are now using us for their own "selfish" purposes, as Richard Dawkins believes is likely to be the case. But even if this worst-case scenario were true, it still may be the case that *some* religious ideas, *some* religious vocabulary, *some* religious traditions and rituals, and *some* religious symbols, may prove useful for the growth, learning, and the continuing evolution of our species.

Moderate religious thinkers do not think that it is an embarrassment or a cop-out to pick and choose from among the great resources of traditional religious thinking. Moderate religious thinkers do so with great reverence, humility, and care; not doing so blindly and mindlessly, this picking and choosing itself being a time-honored religious practice. It is simply not the case that "Religious moderation is the product of secular knowledge and scriptural ignorance" (2004, 21), as Sam Harris asserts. In fact, his criticism that religious moderates fail "to live by the letter of the text" (21) is a strange complaint coming from an author who rejects literalism and embraces subtlety and irony in expression and thought.

SELF-CONSCIOUS EVOLUTION AND DIALOGUE

From a moderately religious point of view, and from many other points of view for that matter, many of us are coming to realize that the key to our self-conscious evolution is open and ongoing dialogue. This means that we have to learn how to respect one another, listen to one another, and to voice our opinions in an honest and frank way. The goal is not to limit dialogue partners to those with whom we already agree; the goal of dialogue is to embrace the other and to continually widen the circle of dialogue. Through dialogue, we must learn to tolerate strange languages, seemingly odd beliefs, and foreign vocabularies. We must accept that our worldview and our practices are not definitive of "reality" or necessarily the only ones consistent with living a meaningful life. A life committed to dialogue brings an ethical responsibility and a great self-interest to actively seek out dialogue partners and to try to understand them *on their own terms* as best we can, rather than trying to silence them. Dialogue is both the means to and the ends of our moral aspirations and our democratic institutions.

The contemporary Yale University philosopher Seyla Benhabib describes the kind of "communicative ethics" I am calling for here as follows:

> When we shift the burden of the moral test in communicative ethics from consensus to the idea of an ongoing moral conversation, we begin to ask not what all would or could agree to as a result of practical discourses to be morally permissible or impermissible, but what would be allowed and perhaps even necessary from the standpoint of continuing and sustaining the practice of moral conversation among us. The emphasis now is less on *rational agreement*, but more on sustaining those normative practices and moral relationships within which reasoned agreement *as a way of life* can flourish and continue. (Benhabib 1992, 38; emphasis in original)

For Benhabib and others, ethics is not only about the single individual discovering and applying moral principles, or even about individual moral character, but ethics is primarily concerned with both the theoretical and practical problems of "continuing and sustaining the practice of moral conversation among us." In other words, how do we keep the ethical conversations going?

A Change in Consciousness

True dialogue demands a *change in consciousness*. It requires that we finally abandon the quest for certainty. It means that we must give up either/or thinking in favor of both/and thinking. Dialogue means that we must take responsibility for our own actions, including creatively seeking out dialogue partners and not just engaging in the wishful thinking that somehow these partners will magically come around to *our* way of thinking. It means that we cannot simply rely on traditional sources of authority. It embraces paradox and celebrates differences. Through dialogue, participants come to realize that we will not discover a single language that is best for every human purpose, but that different languages and different ways of speaking will be more or less useful depending on our shared aspirations and goals. In dialogue, we must come prepared to learn from one another and be willing to alter even our most cherished beliefs, if this is the reasonable thing to do.

Is this the view of all religious people? Certainly not. But for those of us who believe and put their faith in the efficacy and ethics of dialogue, the only way to convince others to join in is through example and demonstration and not through name-calling or withdrawal.

I believe that the great strength and value of the four books under review is the descriptions these authors provide of this new kind of consciousness necessary for the kinds of *deep* ethical dialogues I am imagining. None of the authors consistently lives and exhibits this new consciousness, nor does anyone else for that matter, but all of them identify and provide apt and useful descriptions of some of the most salient aspects, insights, and attitudes necessary for nurturing and sustaining life-enhancing dialogues. How important is dialogue? It is useful to quote the social entrepreneur Lynne Twist here. "I believe that we don't really live in the world. We live in the conversation we have about that world . . . And over that we have absolute, omnipotent power. We have the opportunity to shape that conversation, and in so doing to shape our history" (as quoted in Brown 2005, 24).

Religious moderates must have the ability and patience to tolerate and remain in the space of dialogue even in the face of unvarnished, exaggerated, and even quite peculiar statements in some cases like Christopher Hitchens's subtitle that "religion poisons everything." *Everything?* Sam Harris writes that "nothing that a Christian and a Muslim can say to each other will render their beliefs mutually vulnerable to discourse" (2004, 46). *Nothing?* Richard Dawkins states flatly that the "God of the Old Testament is arguably the most unpleasant character in all fiction: jealous and proud of it; a petty, unjust, unforgiving control-freak; a vindictive, bloodthirsty ethnic cleanser; a misogynistic, homophobic, racist, infanticidal, genocidal, filicidal, pestilential, megalomaniacal, sadomasochistic, capriciously malevolent bully" (2006, 31). *The most unpleasant character in all of fiction?*

It is difficult to continue to dialogue in the face of these descriptions of one's own "sacred" texts and cherished beliefs. I have no doubt that each of these writers is sincere in his passionate and extreme beliefs, denunciations, and articulations (a moral passion, by the way, one might ironically describe best as biblical in its proportions). This is indeed what radical atheists think about religious thinking, and this is precisely why it is so hard for religious moderates to hear and to tolerate it.

My main claim here, in this review, is that despite all of this hyperbole, inexactness, lack of empathy, lack of toleration, and lack of respect—and be warned, there is *much more* in store for anyone who gets through these jeremiads—religious moderates have much to learn from the new atheists.

RICHARD DAWKINS AND HIS AMAZING ABILITY TO IMAGINE WHAT IT'S LIKE TO BE A BAT

I want to start with Richard Dawkins, an obviously brilliant scientist who has a special knack of being able to explain difficult concepts of Darwinian evolutionary theory in a captivating and understandable way to a wide, general audience. Even Daniel Dennett, a staunch supporter and intellectual ally of Dawkins (he is cited more than thirteen times in Dennett's book while Dawkins cites Dennett twelve times), must admit that Dawkins "is no friend of religion" and describes at least one of Dawkins's more extreme pronouncements as a "jarring claim" (Dawkins 184). Even so, I believe, it is worth reading and listening to what Dawkins has to say in his most recent book.

Consider two of the most difficult obstacles to overcome in engaging in successful dialogue. The first is a kind of unexamined certainty that each of us normally brings to the table. Simply put, we typically think of our own beliefs as mirroring "reality." We believe that our ideas are true in the sense that they correspond in some kind of exact one-to-one fashion to what is out there in the "real" world. This is true, of course, in the domain of science, but it is a particularly troublesome habit of thought in the domain of ethics, especially for those of us who now believe that both the content and authority of ethics is finally determined only through open and uncoerced dialogue.

A second obstacle to overcome, not completely unrelated to the first, is our inability to imagine the world from someone else's point of view. For the most part, it seems as if we are trapped inside of our own heads. It is often hard for us to believe that what we see, what we "know" that we "really" see, is not precisely what our neighbors or enemies see. How does one begin to examine one's own most cherished beliefs? How does one go about holding on to one's own vision of the world and how it works, and, at the very same time, how do we learn to imagine how other people view it? It's almost like being in two places at once, a seeming impossibility.

I do not think that overcoming these obstacles is simply a matter of more and better knowledge. Rather, overcoming these obstacles to dialogue demands a new kind of awareness or, more precisely, a new and enlarged kind of ethical consciousness. This new consciousness is hard to come by, and when a respected scientist begins to describe it *from the inside*, it is worth lining up and listening to. Here is Dawkins, at his best, in his own words: "'Really' isn't a word we should use with simple confidence. If a neutrino had a brain which had evolved in neutrino-sized ancestors, it would say that rocks 'really' do consist mostly of empty space. We have brains that evolved in medium-sized ancestors, who couldn't walk through rocks, so our 'really' is a 'really' in which rocks are solid. 'Really,' for an animal is whatever its brain needs it to be, in order to assist its survival. And because different species live in such different worlds, there will be a troubling variety of 'reallys'" (Dawkins). Dawkins continues in the best tradition of the philosophical pragmatism of William James and John Dewey: "What we see of the real world is not the unvarnished real world but a *model* of the real world, regulated and adjusted by sense data—a model that is constructed so that it is useful for dealing with the real world. The nature of that model depends on the kind of animals we are. A flying animal needs a different kind of model from prey, even though their worlds necessarily overlap. A monkey's brain must have software capable of stimulating a three-dimensional maze of branches and trunks" (2006, 371–72). These are extremely useful insights to keep in mind as we argue and debate with one another in the context of dialogue. Participants, whether discussing scientific truths, the nature of beauty, or the role of religion in society, would benefit greatly from keeping in mind, especially in the heat of the moment, that we are not arguing about reality as such, but we are arguing about our "models"—to use Dawkins helpful term—of reality. This may be a subtle difference, but it is an important and extremely hard-won difference.

Our dialogues, regardless of the topic, should focus on which model is more appropriate or which model is most useful *for the purposes and human problems at hand*. We should give up the attempt to find a language that tells us *how it is* regardless of *what it is that we need and want*. Every conceivable model of reality must ultimately be judged in terms of what it gets us, where it takes us, or its "cash value," as William James put it more than a century ago (James 1991). A dialogue based on which model is most appropriate (or even just appropriate enough) for a given purpose will be more prosaic, down to earth, less heated, and more productive than our typical historical disagreements about the nature of reality, especially when it comes to theological disagreements.

It was observed above that dialogue requires an ability to imagine the world from someone else's point of view. Even if we can come to appreciate that what we are arguing and debating is not about reality in itself but our models of reality, to engage in deep dialogue we still need to find ways to imagine what these other models look and feel like from inside one another's perspectives. Dawkins in the continuation of the discussion quoted above claims—and to my mind successfully demonstrates—that we can *on occasion* do exactly this. Amazingly, Dawkins demonstrates his ability not only to imagine the inner life of other human interlocutors, but he shows that it is possible for us to imagine what is going on inside the minds of other species, as well. Dawkins makes the imaginative leap from human to bat. Just as our visual perception includes different colors because this has served an evolutionary function, so too bats, he imagines, "hear" different "colors." Here is how Dawkins describes all of this:

> The world-model that a bat needs, in order to navigate through three dimensions catching insects, must surely be similar to the model that a swallow needs in order to perform much the same task. The fact that the bat uses echoes to update the variables in his model, while the swallow uses light, is incidental. Bats, I suggest, use perceived hues such as "red" and "blue" as internal labels for some useful aspects of echoes, perhaps the acoustic texture of surfaces; just as swallows use the same perceived hues to label long and short wavelengths of light. The point is that the nature of the model is governed by how it is to be *used* rather than by the sensory modality involved. The lesson of the bats is this. The general form of the mind model—as opposed to the variables that are constantly being inputted by sensory nerves—is an adaptation to the animal's way of life, no less than its wings, legs and tails are. (372)

This is a neat trick that Dawkins is pulling off here. What *is it* like to be a bat or any other animal for that matter? Dawkins is not just providing us with more scientific knowledge through this example, he is demonstrating an entirely new method of thinking. He is expanding and deepening his own consciousness—one might say he is becoming *self-reflective*—in order to understand the consciousness, in some small way, of a different species of animal. This imaginative leap is exactly what all of us must learn how to do, as a matter of course, to participate fully in effective dialogue.

Had Dawkins used this same self-reflective ability to imagine what it is like—not to be a bat, but to be a religious person—would he have used the same kind of rhetoric and reached some of the same seemingly radical conclusions that he does reach in his book? For example, would Dawkins continue to claim that damage from sexual abuse by Catholic priests "is arguably less than the long-term psychological damage inflicted by bringing the child up Catholic in the first place" (317)? This is an outrageous and inflammatory comment with absolutely no scientific justification whatsoever to back it up (this may, in fact, have been Dawkins's experience, but his own personal experience is almost certainly not the norm). Dawkins's own qualification that "this was an off-the-cuff remark made in the heat of the moment" hardly excuses him from the fact that he seemingly proudly repeats this comment a second time in the more sober context of his best-selling book. Does Dawkins ever begin to wonder how this sounds inside the head of a religious Catholic? Would he describe Judaism as "originally a tribal cult of a fiercely unpleasant God, morbidly obsessed with sexual restrictions, with the smell of charred flesh, with his own superiority over other gods and with the exclusiveness of his chosen desert tribe" if he imagined these comments from a Jewish point of view? (37) Perhaps, but I'd like to think not.

We can learn something important even from Dawkins's mistakes, though. The new kind of expanded consciousness that dialogue demands is not learned once and for all and then applied universally. We should stop thinking of it as a permanent developmental accomplishment. This is probably asking too much from anyone. It is something that all of us learn, forget, and then relearn. It is something that we apply on an ad hoc basis, unevenly and unfairly, rather than systematically across all domains. It is an ability that requires constant awareness and mindfulness. It is a skill that, in the name of dialogue, both those of us who invoke God's name and those of us who choose not to invoke God's name must begin to foster with extreme care and attention.

Might it just not be the case that when atheists look out and see the world that the "colors" they see are of a slightly different hue than the "colors" religious believers see? Atheists and believers are using different languages and different vocabularies, but, for the most part, they are using them for altogether different purposes. To the extent that this may now be creating more problems than it is solving, the new atheists are quite correct to demand more and better accountability from religious believers. But accountability is really just another aspect of what it means to be in dialogue, and all of us, believers and nonbelievers alike, now possess an emerging responsibility for far more and better accountability to one another than ever before.

SAM HARRIS AND THE WILLINGNESS TO HAVE OUR BELIEFS MODIFIED BY NEW FACTS

A central element to the developing consciousness being described here is the human ability to take in new facts, learn new information, build new theoretical models, and evolve in the face of ever-changing environments. These modes of thinking are necessary to *jump-start* dialogues in the first place, and yet they are also skills and modes of thinking that will be honed and improved *through participating* in dialogues of the sort contemplated here. Sam Harris provides a clear statement of what I am talking about: "It is time we recognized that the only thing that permits human beings to collaborate with one another in a truly open-ended way is their willingness to have their beliefs modified by new facts. Only openness to evidence and argument will secure a common world for us. Nothing guarantees that reasonable people will agree about everything, of course, but the unreasonable are certain to be divided by their dogmas" (48). This ability to "collaborate with one another in a truly open-ended way" to create a "common world" is not primarily about acquiring new techniques and specific skills, but this ability is central to our very identity as persons. Harris is quite correct here when he introduces the notion of consciousness as playing the critical role in human development. "Our spiritual traditions suggest that we have considerable room here to change our relationship to the contents of consciousness, and thereby to transform our experience of the world. Indeed, a vast literature on human spirituality attests to this. It is also clear that nothing need be believed on insufficient evidence for us to look into this possibility with an open mind" (207). One of Harris's most important insights with regard to coming to a deeper understanding and appreciation of our own consciousness is his claim "that the feeling of self is best thought of as a *process*" (212). To understand this, Harris elaborates as follows: "Look at this book as a physical object. You are aware *of* it as an appearance in consciousness. You may feel that your consciousness is one thing—it is whatever illuminates your world from some point behind your eyes, perhaps—and the book is another. This is the kind of dualistic (subject/object) perception that characterizes our normal experiences of life. It is possible, however, to look for your self in such a way as to put this subject/object dichotomy in doubt—and even to banish it altogether" (213). To my mind, Harris draws the correct *ethical* conclusion from his new discovery. "Clearly, there is nothing optimal—or even necessarily *viable*—about our present form of subjectivity. Almost every problem we have can be ascribed to the fact that human beings are utterly beguiled by their feelings of separateness. It would seem that a spirituality that undermined such dualism, through the mere contemplation of consciousness, could not help but improve our situation" (214).

I could not agree more with this last quote from Harris. In order to promote ethical dialogue and to achieve a kind of "meeting of minds," whether we are talking about scientific, aesthetic, ethical, or religious concerns, our ability to move beyond these beguiling "feelings of separateness" is crucial. It may turn out that there really is no "us versus them" or "believers versus atheists" in any kind of fundamental or real sense. These are just words we use—human tools—to invent novel sentences, more or less usefully, depending on the purposes and problems at hand.

Does Harris himself understand completely the profound and world-shattering implications of his own emerging insights? Are the differences between atheists and believers as weighty and substantial as he makes them out to be? Is it really the case that "there is clearly no greater obstacle to a truly empirical approach to spiritual experience than our current beliefs about God"? (214). It may very well be true that an unexamined acceptance of a supernatural being is one obstacle to spiritual experience. I, in fact, agree with this last proposition, but no doubt, there are many other obstacles as well. The single-minded quest for ever-increasing profits and growth on the part of global corporations to the neglect of corporate social responsibility, the mindless destruction of our fragile environment, the inexcusable condition of poor people around the world, and the *unaccountable* pursuit of science and technology are four examples that come quickly to mind.

Earlier in his book, Harris stumbles badly and reverts to a much more traditional state of consciousness, the very same consciousness he battles so successfully in the material quoted above from the last part of his book. Consider how far the following description is from both Dawkins's view (as cited above) and even Harris himself:

> Our statements about the world will be "true" or "false" not merely in virtue of how they function amid the welter of our other beliefs, or with reference to any culture-bound criteria, but because reality simply *is* a certain way, independent of our thoughts. Realists believe that there

are truths about the world that may exceed our capacity to know them; there are facts of the matter whether or not we can bring such facts into view. To be an ethical realist is to believe that in ethics, as in physics, there are truths waiting to be *discovered*—and thus we can be right or wrong about our beliefs in them. (181)

In Harris's view, he has already *discovered* many of these truths: Harris opposes "religious tolerance" and does not believe that individuals should be "free to believe whatever they want about God" (15). Presumably, we can only believe what Harris has already discovered to be the case. Much more troubling than this, however, is Harris's contention that we—just who "we" is is not always clear—may have an obligation to *kill* people for their "wrong" beliefs. "Some propositions are so dangerous that it may even be ethical to kill people for believing them. This may seem an extraordinary claim, but it merely enunciates an ordinary fact about the world in which we live. Certain beliefs place their adherents beyond the reach of every peaceful means of persuasion, while inspiring them to commit acts of extraordinary violence against others" (52–53).

There is an incredible irony, here, of course. *These* beliefs of Harris are exactly the beliefs (might one be entitled to call them pernicious memes?) that so many religious moderates have been struggling to *overcome* for so long. In many religions, in fact, *these are* the traditional beliefs. Harris himself is trapped inside a worldview or a "mind model" to borrow Dawkins's phrase, from which he is *trying* to escape. In some cases, he is quite successful, and in others he is woefully and dangerously inadequate.

At one point in the book, Sam Harris suggests that the future of our existence is dependent on moderate Muslims. "It does not seem much of an exaggeration to say that the fate of civilization lies largely in the hands of 'moderate' Muslims. Unless Muslims can reshape their religion into an ideology that is basically benign—or outgrow it altogether—it is difficult to see how Islam and the West can avoid falling into a continual state of war on innumerable fronts" (152). I *agree* with this statement, but I don't believe that the kind of book that Sam Harris has written will help strengthen religious moderates vis-à-vis their fundamentalist counterparts. It hardly seems likely that one is going to convince religious fundamentalists to stop killing one another merely in the name of their beliefs by endorsing *exactly* this claim for ourselves!

There is a strange extremism to Harris's writing. One senses an almost paralyzing fear and anxiousness to his style and tone. There is a lack of the kind of deep acceptance—to accept what is, especially when we don't like it—that the writer Jon Kabat-Zinn refers to in his book *Coming to Our Senses* (see especially pp. 407–9). There is an appreciation for *all* of the cultural gifts that we have inherited that is tragically missing here. If civil dialogue is the goal, if we are to learn how to sit and reason together—all of us and not just some of us—about the "sacred dimension to our existence," much of what Harris is explicitly stating is, at best, counterintuitive, and, at worst, counterproductive.

The philosopher John Dewey once said that "the great enemy to what is attainable in happiness in the life of human beings is the attitude of fear" (Dewey, as quoted in Rockefeller 1991, 553). This fear permeates Harris's book. As Dewey further explains this species of fear, "It is an attitude of withdrawal, an attitude of exclusiveness which shuts out the beauties and troubles of experience as the things from which we alone can really learn and go on growing" (ibid).

In a later essay, Dewey expounded further: "Living as we now do in what is almost a chronic state of crisis, there is danger that fear and the sense of insecurity becomes the predominant motivation for our activities . . . Far more than anything else, the fear that has no recognized and well-thought-out ground is what both holds us back and conducts us into aimless and spasmodic ways of action, personal and collective" (ibid). It *is* true that Harris and all of us have much to fear. The question, though, is what can we *do* with this fear? It hardly seems appropriate to blame all of the ills of this world on religion and, in Harris's case, religious moderates. "Religious moderates are, in large part, responsible for the religious conflict in our world, because their beliefs provide the context in which scriptural literalism and religious violence can never be adequately opposed" (45). The worst thing that we can do is to conduct ourselves "into aimless and spasmodic ways of action." Is Harris falling into the trap that Dewey warned us about?

Harris does give us a glimpse at a possible solution. In calling for a new kind of spirituality—"the mere contemplation of consciousness"—that attempts to break the beguiling "feelings of separateness," Harris is describing a new way of being in the world, a new way of relating to the world, a mechanism of perhaps overcoming our unnamed fear. It is only through creating an environment conducive to achieving this kind of expanded consciousness on a more fixed and dependable basis that the crisis that Harris, Dennett, Dawkins, and Hitchens feel so intensely and passionately can be faced.

Sam Harris, I believe in spite of his own rhetoric, is moving, ultimately, in the right direction and he has many insights and ideas worth contemplating. He is probably as ambivalent, anxious, scared, and uncertain as any of us about the future of dialogue and the ability and ultimate effectiveness of speaking truth to power. If there is a positive meaning and purpose to *faith* in the new century, it is this faith in our ability to resolve seemingly intractable conflicts through nonviolent interchange, civil discourse, to "collaborate with one another in a truly open-ended way," that is most worth reconstructing, preserving, and passing along to the next generation.

Christopher Hitchens and the Limits of My Own Thesis

It is my contention in this chapter that religious moderates have much to learn from the new atheists despite some of the exaggerated rhetoric and blind spots they exhibit. Further, I am arguing that each of the four authors under consideration demonstrates and describes the contours of a mature and new kind of consciousness necessary for the kinds of *deep* ethical dialogues I am imagining and advocating. Christopher Hitchens, far more than Harris, Dennett, and Dawkins, tests the limits of my thesis. His book, in fact, although usually lumped together with these others, really stands alone, or at least, *should* stand alone.

Hitchens is unrelenting from the get-go. If it is true that Richard Dawkins is "no friend of religion," as Daniel Dennett put it, how shall we describe Hitchens and his relationship to organized religion? The following excerpt is one random example of the kinds of things that Hitchens has to say about religion on almost every page of his book: "Violent, irrational, intolerant, allied to racism and tribalism and bigotry, invested in ignorance and hostile to free inquiry, contemptuous of women and coercive toward children: organized religion ought to have a great deal on its conscience. There is one more charge to be added to the bill of indictment. With a necessary part of its collective mind religion looks forward to the destruction of the world . . . I mean . . . it openly or covertly wishes that end to occur" (56). I consider myself to be a religious person and a member in good standing of an organized religion, and I, for one, do not subscribe to any of this. I try as hard as I can to avoid violence, irrationality, intolerance, racism, ignorance, contempt of women, and coerciveness toward children. I *support* free speech. I certainly do *not* look forward to the destruction of the world, *nor* do I covertly wish that end to occur! Nor do most of my religious friends. I would think that this should go without saying, but apparently it no longer does.

In some cases, Hitchens repeats historically antireligious canards. In fact, in at least one instance, he rehearses one of the oldest anti-Semitic lies in existence. "Orthodox Jews conduct congress by means of a hole in the sheet," writes Hitchens with no proof or authority because there is no proof or authority.

The list of Hitchens's unfounded diatribes against religion might be almost as long has his entire book. From a Jewish point of view, I would have found his final attack against Judaism's minor holiday of Hannukah to be almost oddly amusing, if I wasn't convinced that he was humorless and deadly serious in this observation. "If one could nominate an absolutely tragic day in human history, it would be the occasion that is now commemorated by the vapid and annoying holiday known as 'Hannukah'" (273). Really? What's the punch line here?

On the very last page of his book, Hitchens calls on us to "banish all religions from the discourse" (283). How he proposes to implement this drastic solution, he doesn't tell us. In any event, this proposal is sharply at odds with the best contemporary philosophical writings on liberalism and democracy. Consider the evolving thought of the world-class philosopher Jurgen Habermas:

> The liberal state has an interest in unleashing religious voices in the political public sphere, and in the political participation of religious organizations as well. It must not discourage religious persons and and communities from also expressing themselves politically *as such*, for it cannot know whether secular society would not otherwise cut itself off from key resources for the creation of meaning and identity. Secular citizens or those of other religious persuasions can under certain circumstances learn something from religious contributions; this is, for example, the case if they recognized normative truth content of a religious utterance hidden intuitions of their own. (2006, 10)

Habermas is not calling for the abolition of the quite sensible and historically viable separation of church and state. He is careful, in several places, to make a sharp distinction between "politicians and officials within political institutions" who must formulate and "justify laws, court rulings, decrees and measures only in a language which is equally accessible to all citizens" and "citizens, political parties and their candidates, social organizations, churches and other religious associations" (6) who are entitled to use a much broader set of reasons and languages.

In the final analysis, Habermas reaches a very different conclusion than Hitchens's radical "banish all religions" principle. In fact, almost anticipating him and others like him, Habermas writes that "secular citizens must open their minds to the possible truth content" of the arguments put forth by religious citizens even when religious citizens are couching these arguments in purely religious language. "Citizens of a democratic community owe one another good reasons for their political statements and attitudes. Even if the religious contributions are not subjected to self-censorship, they depend on the cooperative acts of translation. For without a successful translation there is no prospect of the substantive content of religious voices being taken up in the agendas and negotiations within political bodies and in the broader political process" (11). Democratic ethics demands a heavy cognitive burden, a change in consciousness in my terminology, for all citizens—believers and nonbelievers alike, according Habermas. "What we must expect of the secular citizens is moreover a self-reflective transcending of a secularist self-understanding of Modernity . . . The secular citizens must grasp their conflict with religious opinions as a *reasonably expected disagreement* . . . An epistemic mindset is presupposed here that would originate from a self-critical assessment of the limits of secular reason" (15; emphasis in original).

This change in consciousness is not something that citizens can assume as a matter of course. It will require a joint effort on the part of both believers and nonbelievers. It will not happen all at once, nor once it happens will it be secure once and for all. Education for dialogue will need to be institutionalized and commonplace.

This growth in consciousness is cognitively demanding as Habermas correctly emphasizes, but it is emotionally challenging, as well. Moving into a new way of seeing the world and relating to it, learning to make meaning in a wholly novel way, is not something that is achieved cost-free, nor should it be advertised as such. Moving *into* new ways of seeing the world implies *moving out* of our old ways. This hurts.

The educator Sharon Daloz Parks describes this movement as the "suffering of adult faith." Specifically, she locates this suffering "in learning how to hold on to, and when to let go of, the perceptions, patterns, and relationships that one experiences as partaking in ultimate value and truth" (2000, 33).

This brings me back to, at least, one important contribution of Christopher Hitchens. In a highly useful section of his book, Hitchens describes the growing pains he felt and endured in his own movement away from the almost all-consuming communist ideology of his youth.

When I was a Marxist, I did not hold my opinions as a matter of faith but I did have the conviction that a sort of unified field theory might have been discovered. The concept of historical and dialectical materialism was not an absolute end and it did not have any supernatural element, but it did have its messianic element in the idea that an ultimate moment might arrive, and it most certainly had its martyrs and saints and doctrinaires and (after a while) its mutually excommunicating rival papacies. It also had its schisms and inquisitions and heresy hunts. (2007, 151)

At a later point in his life, however, Hitchens describes to the reader how he was able to emerge from this ideological cocoon, presumably with a deeper consciousness and altered relationship to his own tightly held, but now outmoded, mind model. "Those of us who had sought a rational alternative to religion had reached a terminus that was comparably dogmatic." Is this recognition the seed of Habermas's "epistemic mindset" that originates "from a self-critical assessment of the limits of secular reason"? Hitchens continues in this reflective, nostalgic, but honest manner: "There are days when I miss my old convictions as if they were an amputated limb. But in general I feel better, and no less radical" (153).

In order to advance civil dialogue and the democratic institutions that it supports, *all* of us will have to learn to tolerate the trials and mixed emotions of moving on. We will need to learn how to embrace ambiguity, tolerate uncertainty, and accept and embrace a deep interdependence. We will need to undergo the kind of "conversion" experience Hitchens describes so well on a much more regular basis and at even deeper levels of meaning and significance.

Hitchens, like the rest of us, possesses an important piece of our puzzle. His passion is authentic, his voice is shrill and contrary, his vision is sensitive, and his experiences are real and as valuable as any of ours. True dialogue must contain and tolerate all of this mixed bag. Believers must come to understand not only the intellectual arguments in favor of atheism, but believers also must come to appreciate what it feels like to be an atheist in our culture at this particular moment in time. Hitchens's almost unabated anger is certainly useful for this task. He is trying to warn us, and it behooves us to try and hear him as best we can. In the end, it is not us versus them, but it is all of us working and reasoning together, and searching for good enough words, sentences, and ideas—new and improved memes—to replace our unconscious penchant for force and terror. This is certainly an aspiration all of us, from Hitchens to the religious fundamentalists, can and must work for together.

Daniel Dennett and Capacity for Moral Thinking

Michael Novak, in his review of the new atheists, quickly dismisses the philosopher Daniel Dennett. Novak brusquely states that Dennett "in the guise of studying religion objectively, dismisses it" (2007, 35). This curt conclusion, however, should not be the final word on Dennett.

Of the four books under review, Dennett's is by far the most respectful, least anxious and hysterical, and best written. I believe, contrary to Novak, that this book has the most to contribute to the ongoing dialogue between believers and atheists, and is most likely to achieve its author's intended goal of promoting more civil and reasonable discussions among us—of "breaking the spell," in the words of Dennett's title. Unlike Sam Harris and Richard Dawkins (who are both quoted approvingly in Dennett's book and unfortunately are never challenged) and Christopher Hitchens (who is not quoted in Dennett's book at all), Dennett finds much to praise in religion.

It seems almost silly to quote some of these statements on Dennett's behalf because they would seem to be so self-evident to most readers. But, in light of what Dawkins, Harris, and especially Hitchens have explicitly written, it becomes necessary.

> The daily actions of religious people have accomplished uncounted good deeds throughout history, alleviating suffering, feeding the hungry, caring for the sick. (Dennett 2006, 253)
>
> Religions have brought the comfort of belonging and companionship to many who would have passed through this life alone . . . They have not just provided first aid, in effect, for people in difficulties; they have provided the means for changing the world in ways that remove those difficulties. (ibid)
>
> There is growing evidence that religions have succeeded remarkably well on this score [improving health]. (ibid, 272)
>
> Many deeply religious people have all along been eager to defend their convictions in the court of reasonable inquiry and persuasion. (ibid, 297)
>
> Every religion—aside from a negligible scattering of truly toxic cults—has a population of ecumenical-minded people who are eager to reach out to people of other faiths or no faith at all, and consider the moral quandaries of the world on a rational basis. (ibid)

Even the God of the "Old Testament" evolves from Dawkins's "most unpleasant character in all fiction" to Dennett's "fascinating participant in [the] stories" of the Bible (265). Dennett never jettisons his faith in democratic liberalism, nor does he give up on his fellow human beings, no matter how religious they are. He disavows Sam Harris's "ethical realism" in noting that when it comes time to answering questions about ultimate values, "no factual investigation" can answer them (14). He admits openly that even atheists can have "sacred values that are simply not up for re-evaluation" (23). Dennett's book is so different than Hitchens's that it is unfair how often they are spoken of in the same breath. A quick Internet search discovered more than 50,000 Web pages where their names appear together (June 28, 2007).

Dennett is not immune from hyperbole and contradiction and, at least in one case, outright silliness. One of his definitions of religion, for example, is that for something to be a religion it *must* contain "the postulation of invisible, undetectable effects that . . . are *systematically* immune to confirmation or disconfirmation." He continues, "no religion lacks them, and anything that lacks them is not really a religion, however much it is like a religion in other regards" (164). What happened to all those religions that "consider the moral quandaries of the world on a rational basis" that we just heard about?

Dennett's decision to continue calling himself a "bright" because of his atheistic beliefs seems like it is something less than a serious contribution to the ethical dialogue between believers and atheists in which he is such an important contributor. The term "brights" sounds to me more like the name of a high school club for socially inept adolescents or some kind of incredibly nerdy urban gang than the name acclaimed scientists, philosophers, and journalists would want to self-consciously adopt for themselves. He is right, of course, it is a very "nice word with positive connotations," but this observation is most definitely beside the point. Dennett's invitation to us non-brights, to coin our own endearing term, doesn't make anything better and, I confidently predict, will have few takers.

These, however, are minor complaints, quibbles really, and are hardly worth mentioning. Dennett is a first-rate philosopher, even if he cannot resist a mischievous temptation to tweak us believers now and again. This is something we are all entitled to do, I suppose, and it is something we probably deserve from time to time, as well. While dialogue is certainly a serious matter, it must find a place for gentle (and, on occasion, not so gentle) humor, too.

One of the key differences between Dennett and his fellow atheists is his ability to sustain *more regularly* the deeper consciousness that is so necessary to keep the conversations going even between those of us with profound disagreements. Obviously, one of the single most important questions facing advocates of reasonable dialogue is if it is really possible for us to overcome our own inherent self-interest. Can the individual human mind begin to conceive of its own identity primarily as part of—as a component to—some more inclusive identity? Or, are we doomed to imagine ourselves as locked in a struggle of competing and mutually exclusive interests? At the end of the day, is dialogue merely the servant of power, or, alternatively, can we meaningfully reconceive power as the handmaiden of dialogue?

> Whenever an agent—an intentional system, in my terminology—makes a decision about the best course of action, all things considered, we can ask from whose perspective this optimality is being judged. A more or less standard default assumption, at least in the Western world, and especially among economists, is to treat each human agent as a sort of isolated and individualistic locus of well-being. What's in it for *me*? Rational *self*-interest. But although there has to be something in the role of the self—something that answers the *cui bono*? question for decision-maker under examination—there is no necessity in this default treatment, common as it is. (Dennett 2006, 176)

This is a breakthrough in consciousness being described here by Dennett. In his words, "there is no *necessity* in this default treatment." But if Dennett is right and the "self" is not necessarily "me" or "I," then what is it? Here is Dennett's answer:

> A self-as-ultimate-beneficiary can in principle be indefinitely distributed in space and time. I can care for others, or for a larger social structure, for instance. There is nothing that restricts me to a *me* as contrasted to an *us*. I can still take my task to be looking out for Number One while including, under Number One, not just myself, and not just my family, but also Islam, or Oxfam, or the Chicago Bulls! The possibility, opened up by cultural evolution, of installing such novel perspectives in our brains is what gives our species, and only our species, the capacity for moral—and immoral thinking. (176)

There is a level of consciousness, a way of being in the world, Dennett promises, that allows us to overcome narcissism, to jettison individual self-interest, to reexperience ourselves as interconnected beings and not as atomistic, isolated, individuals. There is a genuine and authentic state of mind beyond our "default" condition of always asking, "What's in it for me?"

It is hard for me to imagine that anyone can live in this place permanently, nor would we necessarily want to, but to strengthen our faith in dialogue, it is useful to remind ourselves that many of us can, at least, temporarily find refuge in an alternative worldscape. Hardened assumptions of us versus them can melt away almost immediately through the kind of mind-shift Dennett is talking about.

The fear and anxiety that atheists experience is the same fear and anxiety that believers experience. The hate and the love all of us feel (at least sometimes) does not belong solely to you or to me, but the hatred and the love is part of *who we all are*. In the moment of dialogue, we are not only Muslims, Christians, Jews, Buddhists, Hindus, agnostics, or atheists; we are simultaneously a community of one, a solidarity, or at least this is the imagined image. In the moment of dialogue, we escape the trap of our own self-imposed descriptions. We continue to inhabit our own identities, but more casually and less seriously. In the moment of dialogue, we allow ourselves to grow together and to discover a far more complex and beautiful world than we could ever have perceived standing alone, isolated. "We are, as it were, introduced into a world beyond this world which is nevertheless the deeper reality of the world in which we live in our ordinary experience" (Dewey, as quoted by Rockefeller 1991, 509). In these reverential moments many of us can affirm hand in hand with the uncompromising and unapologetic atheist philosopher Daniel Dennett that "the world is sacred" (2006, 245).

The Role of Religious Moderates

Not everyone agrees with the new atheists that there exists a huge gap between the values of believers and nonbelievers. Charles Taylor, the eminent philosopher, for example, writes that "there doesn't seem to be an important conflict here. We agree surprisingly well, across great differences of theological and metaphysical belief, about the demands of justice and benevolence, and their importance. There are differences, including the stridently debated one about abortion. But the very rarity of these cases, which contributes to their saliency, is eloquent testimony to the general agreement" (1989, 515). Is Taylor's pre-9/11 optimistic pronouncement dated? Perhaps it is more wishful thinking than anything else; nonetheless, it remains an inspiring vision to keep hold of, to guide us, as we continue this discussion.

Perhaps the single most important challenge these atheists have put forth in their new books is the assertion that religious moderates will need to play *the* significant role in healing the rifts created by the ascendancy of radical religious fundamentalism throughout the world. The atheists assert a special responsibility for religious moderates in this task. Simply by virtue of the fact that we publicly identify as

Jews, Christians, and Muslims, the atheists argue, we necessarily take on an added moral responsibility "to desanctify the excesses in each tradition *from the inside*" (Dennett 2006, 301; emphasis in original). Further, only those of us who continue to profess a belief in God can, from a practical point of view, effectively tone down the irrational and explosive exuberances and beliefs of our fundamentalist religious brothers and sisters.

Let us imagine religious moderates stepping up to the plate and accepting this challenge. It is highly doubtful that Dennett's suggestion to name names and "out" the worst villains here would really get us to where we want to go. This suggestion is simply a call for more of the same kinds of things all of us, on all sides, are already doing with no cajoling even necessary. And it is simply not working.

Rather, I suggest we begin to remind ourselves that to make lasting changes in the world out there, we must begin by changing our own selves first (Quinn 2004). This means we need to change not only our outward behavior, but we also must alter the very way we make meaning in the world. In other words, we must continue to develop the quality of our own consciousnesses.

Can religious moderates accept the fact that when we engage in debates and arguments with one another that we are not really arguing about reality as such but our models of reality? Can religious moderates begin to imagine what the world looks and feels like from points of view other than our own religiously moderate one? Can we advance beyond the dualisms of subject/object thinking? Can we resist the beguiling temptations of separateness? Can we tolerate the anxiety, pain, and uncertainty of moral growth? And, finally, can we begin to experience our own identities as both a "we" and "I" simultaneously?

While I do not think that the majority of religious moderates can answer these questions in the affirmative, I have no doubt that there are *some* religiously moderate people who can answer yes to all of these questions (at least for the most part). In the Jewish world that I am most familiar with, people like David Hartman, Yitz and Blu Greenberg, Norman Lamm, Saul Berman, Aviva Zornberg, Jonathan Sacks, Harold Schulweis, Tamar Ross, Eugene Borowitz, Harold S. Kushner, and Natan Sharansky come to mind quickly. These are all rabbis, leaders, writers, and/or thinkers who have deeply influenced my own worldview. They have done this not only through their religious and philosophical writings but also through the exemplary lives each one of them lives and the tremendous accomplishments and *mitzvot* (good deeds) each of them has achieved.

These believers are nothing like the one-dimensional caricatures quickly drawn and easily dismissed by Harris, Dawkins, and especially Christopher Hitchens. All of these thinkers are engaged, not in the task of tearing others down, but in the creative task of discovering and inventing meaningful and significant modes of living. Their spirituality is "the thoughtful love of life" that the skeptic philosopher Robert Solomon describes so well (Solomon 2002, 6). They are like artists producing wonderful and inspiring tapestries to be enjoyed, studied, and appreciated. They are storytellers that give life depth, nuance, and flow. They are musicians that help us hear the melodies and rhythms that make our lives more tolerable. They provide us with alternative ways of looking at our world beyond the crass commercialism that is found literally everywhere today.

They are teachers handing over to us some of the ancient moral resources that can sustain, hold, and inspire us especially in times of crisis and despair. They connect us to our past and point us to a better future. They are the role models that religious moderates, at their best, strive to emulate. None of these people invoke a special and unaccountable kind of authority. Their authority, to the extent that they *are* authoritative in some ways, is derived exclusively from their special expertise and their achievements in developing their characters and levels of consciousness to the fullest potential.

I am not sure that atheists should expect much more from religious moderates other than to pick their role models mindfully and then to listen harder and more carefully to what they are actually saying (not what we think they are saying). It seems to me that what the atheists are asking for from religious moderates, to the extent that it goes beyond opening ourselves up to the potential of dialogue, is a species of magical thinking. Religious moderates, just like Dennett, Dawkins, Harris, and Hitchens, abhor force and violence. The overriding goal at this point is to keep the ethical conversations going.

Is God Really the Deal Breaker?

I suggest we look for ways to finesse our differences rather than emphasize them. The call of the hour is for tact and diplomatic maneuvering and not bullying and clubbing each other over the head just because we are using the wrong words at the wrong time.

Is God really the deal breaker, as the atheists imagine? Is God the bright red line that divides people into us and them? And, if so, does it always have to be this way? I believe, perhaps with not quite enough evidence as I need and as I would like to have yet, that this is a choice that both believers and atheists can make together.

It is useful to recall Dawkins at this point. We don't have direct knowledge of reality; we only have direct knowledge of our models of reality. So, it may turn out, if he is right, that we are not even arguing about the actual existence of God at all (we never were because we cannot), but we are arguing about whether or not it makes practical sense to incorporate this particular term, this concept, in our model of reality. This is a much more prosaic kind of debate, and it is one that is potentially much more fruitful.

The atheists state that religion, to be true to itself, *must* include a belief in a supernatural divine being, a personal God who created the world and continues to interact with it. Then they go on to show, not at all surprisingly, by the way, that such a belief cannot stand up to the assumptions of a naturalistic worldview that by construction excludes supernaturalism in the first place. How *could* it stand up to this kind of logic? I wonder.

My point is that we should be less exacting and demanding in how we define God and more tolerant of different viewpoints for the very simple and practical reason that, in this way, we can continue to experiment and keep the conversations going. Ambiguity in expression and definition is not necessarily a sign of intellectual softness, for one might choose ambiguity purposely as a sign of intellectual maturity and wisdom, as a way of promoting inclusiveness rather than exclusiveness. Ambiguity might be interpreted as an invitation and not as a dialogue stopper.

Words are like tools, and different tools serve different purpose. A sharp sword is useful to slay your opponent, but a blunt one might serve better as a symbol of unity. The absence of dialogue is not just silence but terror. In a world as tightly linked as ours is now, we can no longer afford to ignore one another and passively hope for the best. Nor is it tolerable for one group of people, any group really, to say *it*, whatever *it* is, is your problem and your responsibility and not mine.

What Is God Good For?

Be not afraid of life. Believe that life is worth living, and your belief
will help create the fact. The "scientific proof" that you are right
may not be clear before the day of judgment (or some stage of being
which that expression may serve to symbolize) is reached.

—William James, *The Will to Believe*
and Other Essays in Popular Philosophy

John Dewey, of course, was no friend of supernaturalism, absolut-
ism, or authoritarianism, and yet he insisted on his right to continue
to invoke the language of God both in his private poetry and in his
public writings and speeches. In his Terry Lectures delivered at Yale
University, Dewey directly addressed the issue of his continued and
sustained use of the term God:

> A clear and intense conception of a union of ideal ends with actual con-
> ditions is capable of arousing steady emotion. It may be fed by every
> experience, no matter what its material. In a distracted age, the need
> for such an idea is urgent. It can unify interests and energies now dis-
> persed; it can direct action and generate the heat of emotion and the
> light of intelligence. Whether one gives the name "God" to this union,
> operative in thought and action, is a matter for individual decision. But
> the *function* of such a working union of the ideal and actual seems to
> me to be identical with the force that has in fact been attached to the
> conception of God in all the religions that have a spiritual content; and
> a clear idea of that function seems to me urgently needed at the present
> time. (Dewey 1934, 51–52)

Dewey never considered himself an atheist, although he has often been
incorrectly labeled as one. I believe that his measured and thoughtful
decision to continue invoking God's name served for him as an important recognition of democracy's great debt to religion and religious
resources. Dewey had no interest in dramatically cutting himself off
from his own religious heritage and from his fellow religious citizens.

The new atheists, themselves, either consciously or unconsciously
(and it is not always clear which it is) continue to invoke religious
terms like sacred, evil, sin, awe, and acceptance (to name just a few).
These are, of course, all words and concepts with religious pedigrees.
Does it make sense to continue using these terms? Can we simply
unplug them from their original context and still utilize them in a
meaningful way? I believe that, in the interest of sustaining dialogues,
not only *can we*, but *we must*.

From where does the moral passion and energy of Dawkins, Harris, Dennett, and Hitchens come from but from the prophetic writings of the Bible? On a strictly literal level, it is impossible to understand what Hitchens could possibly mean when he says that such and such is a "sin." How can Harris and Dennett invoke the "sacred" when they are writing from a point of view where this term is literally nonsense? Yet, as readers with sympathy and imagination, we think we know what Hitchens is talking about when he uses the word sin, and we even have a sense of what Harris and Dennett may mean by the term sacred, as well. They are, of course, all speaking metaphorically.

Is it really so different though, as the atheists would have us believe, when a religious believer says he professes belief in God? Have not sophisticated religious believers since the time of Maimonides and his negative theology known that *all* God language is metaphorical? Any sentence formulated about God, for a religious believer, must contain an implicit "as if." Here is what Maimonides wrote more than 800 years ago about the use of religious language in his *Guide for the Perplexed*:

> These subtle notions that very clearly elude the mind cannot be considered through the instrumentality of the customary words, which are the greatest among the causes leading unto error. For the bounds of expression in all languages are very narrow indeed, so that we cannot represent this notion to ourselves except through a certain looseness of expression. Thus when we wish to indicate that the deity is not many, the one who makes the statement cannot say anything but that He is one, even though "one" and "many" are some of the subdivisions of quantity. For this reason we give the gist of the notion and give the mind the correct direction toward the true reality of the matter. (as quoted in Seeskin 2000, 34)

We still need to keep this "looseness of expression" in mind—not as a problem to be overcome through the exclusive use of ever more precise and instrumental language—but as a direction toward a possible solution, as we debate among ourselves what it means, or what it might mean, to be believers, agnostics, or atheists.

Daniel Dennett raises the question of whether it is belief in God that matters most to us or is it belief in belief. Perhaps this is the very definition of a religious moderate: one who believes in the belief in God, one who believes in the belief in faith, one who believes in the belief in trust, community, free choice, forgiveness, atonement, Sabbath consciousness, sacredness, sin, covenant, loving kindness, charity, and so many other positive religious values. One can certainly profess a belief in all of these beliefs without possessing knockdown proofs and without intellectual embarrassment.

Paul Woodruff writes in his elegant and beautiful little book that reverence "is the well-developed capacity to have the feelings of awe, respect, and shame when these are the right feelings to have" (2001, 8). Reverence to me seems like another one of the qualities of consciousness that will prove to be necessary to starting and sustaining the kinds of deep, ethical dialogues I have been describing throughout this chapter.

CONCLUSION

In Jewish ethical writing there is a famous statement: "Every controversy that is for the sake of heaven shall in the end lead to a lasting result, but any controversy that is not for the sake of heaven shall not in the end be permanent" (Ethics of the Fathers, Chapter 5, Mishna 17). One simple way of interpreting this statement, useful for my purposes here, is simply that arguments that are intended by the participants in order to uncover truths are of lasting importance and possess intrinsic value, but arguments intended for other purposes besides uncovering truth (power, profits, self-aggrandizement, etc.) are of no lasting worth and possess no intrinsic value.

As sound as this reading is, though, I would like to flip this rabbinic statement around. Every controversy that lasts is for the sake of heaven, but any controversy that is not permanent is not for the sake of heaven. In this reading, the goal is not to come to some final, once and for all agreement on matters of utmost urgency—the truth of the matter—but the goal is a more prosaic and everyday one. Simply put, the goal is—in spite of the anxiety, the beguiling feelings of separateness, uncertainty, terror, fear, and rivers of rage—to keep the conversations going. To do so, as this chapter has pointed out, requires a high degree of mindfulness, patience and toleration, a deepened consciousness, and multiple voices and points of view, from believers to atheists, and all points in between. Sam Harris is right that "there is clearly a *sacred* dimension to our existence." I would only add to this that it is the shared process of dialogue that constitutes a most significant aspect of this "sacred" experience.

PART III

APPLICATIONS OF JEWISH ETHICS AS DIALOGUE

CHAPTER 7

BEYOND THE FLAT WORLD METAPHOR

Society is always trying in some way to grind us down to a single flat surface.

—Oliver Wendell Holmes

We have to be the masters of our imagination, not the prisoners.

—Thomas L. Friedman, *The World Is Flat: A Brief History of the Twenty-first Century*

Imagining the world as flat is a useful way of conceiving the world when navigating local landscapes. Looking at the world around us, the world *is* flat, at least for most of our practical purposes. As curiosity deepens and horizons expand, however, the utility of this metaphor diminishes drastically.

What was once a useful life-sustaining and growth-enhancing way of organizing sense perceptions in order to get from point A to point B (and back home again), in the course of time, becomes debilitating and constricting. In fact, it is precisely this metaphor, this way of making meaning in the world, that holds us back from further explorations and keeps us locked up inside our own local neighborhoods. If new problems require a change in consciousness—a new perspective—we must be willing to sacrifice old metaphors for new ones.

Consider Christopher Columbus, for example. This case is particularly appropriate here because it is with Columbus's "discovery" of the New World that Thomas L. Friedman begins his own (600-page) journey in *The World Is Flat: A Brief History of the Twenty-first Century*. Arguably, Columbus's genius was his ability to recognize that our traditional way of looking at the world—the world is flat—while useful for some purposes, was in his time fast becoming an imprisoning metaphor. "It sure does *seem* like the world is flat," he might have said, "but it's more useful for my new and expanded purposes to imagine it as round. At least, I sure hope so!"

In the end, seizing upon this alternative metaphor allowed Columbus to overcome deep-seated and nearly universally shared primitive fears about traveling too far away from home and falling off the face of the flat world. The new—round world—metaphor opened up new continents, and connected us to new populations and foreign cultures, in ways, good and bad, that no one in Europe before Columbus's imaginative leap could have possibly foreseen. This metaphor enlarged our conception of the world but at the same time made us feel more at home in it and less fearful of it.

With all of this in mind then, Thomas Friedman's choice of the flat-world metaphor is a strange one, especially for a book whose stated purpose is to provide a framework for how to think reasonably about the enormous technological changes that have occurred in the last few years. This task would seem to demand *new* ways of conceiving our world, *new* metaphors to live by, and not a nostalgic embrace of a single outworn way of thinking.

In conceiving of the world as flat, my first association is not with Friedman's brave new technological platform at all. In my mind, the flat-world metaphor immediately conjures up the image of the toppled World Trade Center—two of the proudest and tallest buildings in the world *flattened* in an evil instant, recorded forever on video, and to be replayed over and over as another stark reminder of the plausibility of Nietzsche's "eternal recurrence." As the great nineteenth-century philosopher once wrote, "The life as you now live it and have lived it, you will have to live once more and innumerable times more; and there will be nothing new in it."

WHY USE THE F-WORD?

As one of Friedman's closest readers and most trenchant critics, the UCLA economics professor Edward E. Leamer asks why use the "f-word" at all? After all, he wonders out loud, "What is the alternative to a flat world? A smooth sphere? Bumps?" (2006, 2)

The flat word metaphor, invoked on nearly every page of Friedman's book, serves several different functions simultaneously. According to Friedman, a flat world means

- we are in the process of connecting all the knowledge centers across the planet into a single global network allowing for multiple forms of collaboration,
- common standards are emerging,

- there are fewer and fewer places to hide (thanks to Google and other search engines),
- the world is shrinking,
- we are creating a single and more level playing field,
- hierarchical structures are everywhere giving way to flat forms of organization,
- workers in India flatten their accents and change their names in order to compete more effectively,
- small companies can act big and big companies can act small, and
- machines can talk to other machines with no humans being necessary at all.

There is much more implied in the flat-world metaphor, according to Friedman, but this partial list must suffice for now.

In using this metaphor over and over, Friedman (and the reader) become confused as to whether or not the world is *already* flat (or nearly so) and this is just a plain and simple old fact we will have to learn how to live with somehow, or if this is an enabling and positive vision of what the world might someday become if we play our cards right. There is a continuous flip-flop on this crucial point, and one is suspicious that Friedman himself is not really sure about all of this. On page 232, for example, Friedman breathlessly writes, "The new flat-world platform is, in effect, blowing away our walls, ceiling, and floors—all at the same time. That is, the wiring of the world with fiber-optic cable, the Internet, and work flow software has blown down many of the walls that prevented collaboration. Individuals who never dreamt they could work together, and jobs no one ever dreamt could be shifted from country to country, are suddenly on the move, now that many traditional walls are gone." But then just six pages later, a more sober and realistic Friedman writes, "But we do know that we are all still human beings and human beings need walls, ceilings, and floors—we need agreed-upon norms of behavior and rules of commerce. We need agreed upon ways of establishing authority and building communities, doing work, protecting copyrights, and determining who to trust." The flat-world platform both blows "away our walls, ceiling, and floors," and at the same time this very same flat world demands "walls, ceilings, and floors." Well, which is it?

It is at best unclear how the flat-world metaphor on which Friedman's entire analysis holds together can possibly help us resolve this seeming inconsistency at the heart of his vision. It is not enough to tell us a few hundred pages later that "I have engaged in literary license in titling this book *The World Is Flat*" (461). "I know that the world is *not* flat" (460; emphasis added). It seems like it is far too late in the analysis to finally admit to the reader that "there are hundreds of millions of people on this planet who have been left behind by the flattening process or feel overwhelmed by it, and some of them have enough access to the flattening tools to use them against the system, not on its behalf" (461). By the time one reaches the end of Thomas Friedman's *The World Is Flat*, the metaphor itself has been torn apart by the weight of its own high aspirations. Friedman is trying to squeeze out way too much from his flat-world metaphor.

What Does a Flat World Really Look Like?

On a flat world, gazelles in Africa wake up knowing that they "must run faster than the fastest lion." Lions wake up knowing that they must "outrun the slowest gazelle." And, "It doesn't matter whether you are a lion or a gazelle. When the sun comes up, you better start running" (137).

This is a stark and pessimistic view, but this is cold reality on the flatlands. We better get used to it. Here are some other uncomfortable truths, according to Friedman:

> Each of us, as an individual, will have to work a little harder and run a little faster to keep our standard of living rising. (276)

> The cold, hard truth is that management, shareholders, and investors are largely indifferent to where their profits come from or even where the employment is created. (245)

> When you totally flatten your supply chain you also take a certain element of humanity out of life. (252)

> We should be embarking immediately on an all-hands-on-deck, no-holds barred, no-budget-too-large crash program for science and engineering education. Scientists and engineers don't grow on trees. They have to be educated through a long process. (359)

In Friedman's vision, a flat world is a world where music exists but only to serve the logic of technology and not as an end in itself. It turns out, he explains, that music is a good preparation for a career in science or engineering. I assume Friedman is right about this, but perhaps the meanings and functions of music (and other artistic endeavors) are deeper still.

A flat world is a world where religions serve merely to tie us down to the past and have nothing to offer for the future. Not only is God dead on a flat world, but spirituality is completely missing as well. In a book that describes itself as a "brief history" it is noteworthy to observe that the terms religion and spirituality are not listed at all in the index.

A flat world is a world where every problem one encounters is a technological one and no one ever discovers a technology not to love. On a flat world we share knowledge and information like nobody's business, but there is not a single mention of wisdom, meaning, or understanding. On a flat world, we are seemingly e-mailing and inter-facing with one another all the time, but there is no time left over for open and transformative dialogue. On a flat world, it is not even clear whether or not democracy is truly a positive. At one point, Friedman writes that the fundamental issue in China is not democracy, "the real issue is leadership" (419). Hmmm. Really?

In the last chapter of *The World Is Flat*, Friedman quotes his friend David Rothkopf, a former Commerce Department official. According to Rothkopf, "the real foundation for our security and the real source of our strength" are our deeply held values. Rothkopf continues, "And we need to recognize that our enemies can never defeat us. Only we can defeat ourselves, by throwing out the rule book that has worked for us for a long, long time" (553). Reading this quickly, it seems as though Friedman is quoting his friend because he *agrees* with him. It would seem from this quote that, even on a flat world, technology and social welfare are built on the kind of values human beings choose together and not the other way around.

This, however, is *not* Friedman's point of view at all. He is as clear as he can be on this issue. Earlier in the book Friedman explains to the reader that he has often been charged with the accusation of being a "technological determinist." Quoting his detractors, he writes, "To listen to you, Friedman, there are these ten flatteners, they are con-verging and flattening the earth, and there is nothing that people can do but bow to them and join the parade. After a transition, everyone will get richer and smarter and it will all be fine" (459). To this ques-tion of whether or not he is a technological determinist, Friedman responds in the very next paragraph, "This is a legitimate question, so let me try to answer it directly: *I am a technological determinist! Guilty as charged*" (460; emphasis in original).

So, on a flat world, it turns out, it is *not* values that provide the foundation for technology and social welfare as Rothkopf was quoted above as stating, but it is technology that *determines* values. In one of Friedman's coldest, most macho, and fearsome descriptions of the flat world, he tersely writes, "If you can do it, you must do it, otherwise our competitors will" (460). Remember those lions and gazelles in Africa waking up every morning and running as fast as they possibly can. Well, in a flat world *we* are the lions and gazelles. No wonder Harvard philosopher Michael Sandel compared Friedman's mechanical and deterministic view—"the inexorable march of technology and capital to remove all barriers, boundaries, frictions, and restraints to global commerce" (235)— to Karl Marx's who wrote even more famously than Friedman had.

BEYOND A FLAT WORLD

It is interesting to note that Joseph E. Stiglitz, Nobel Prize–winning economist and one of the leading authorities in the world on globalization, is not mentioned even once in Friedman's book (Aronica and Ramdoo 2006). In his important but much less publicized work, Stiglitz has moved beyond Friedman's simple flat world and all of its implications. According to Stiglitz, it is simply not the case as Friedman (at times) seems to be suggesting that technological breakthroughs inevitably lead to increases in social welfare. "Unfortunately, all that goes under the name of progress does not truly represent progress, even in the narrow economic sense of the term . . . there are innovations, changes in technology, that, while they represent increases in efficiency, *lower* economic well-being, at least for a significant fraction of the population" (2004, 25; emphasis added).

In explicitly rejecting "technological determinism," Stiglitz offers a worldview utterly unlike Friedman's. Contrary to Friedman, Stiglitz states, "We have followed one evolutionary path; there are others. Much of the political and social struggle going on today is an attempt to change that path" (24). In Stiglitz's nondeterministic view, government policies, leadership, and moral values can lead economic development and not just follow from it.

Several economic facts might surprise readers of Friedman's book who come away convinced that indeed the world is flat.

First, even with the tremendous economic development in China and India in the last few years, income distributions are *no* flatter now than they were twenty years ago. Income growth has not occurred uniformly. Half of the world's growth in GDP between 1980 and

2000 originated in only four countries: the United States, Japan, China, and India. "The globe's middle class was left behind, with no income growth over those two difficult decades between the 17th and the 36th percentiles," according to the economist Edward Leamer (2006, 35).

It is simply not the case that the world is getting flatter in terms of income distributions. A second interesting fact is that the world is not getting smaller either. It is still an uncontested economic fact of life that "commerce declines dramatically with distance" (Leamer 2006, 37). Leamer continues by noting that this effect "has not diminished even as transportation costs and communications costs have fallen" (38). Although this finding seems counterintuitive and very much at odds with Friedman's flat world and much of what we read in newspapers and magazines, Leamer explains that "it is the product of the GDPs that accounts for the increase in trans-Pacific trade, not a declining effect of distance" (39).

Third, the magnitude of outsourcing is relatively small. Leamer estimates that the total number of jobs that have actually been outsourced to India lies somewhere between 4,200 and 87,000 jobs. Considering that the U.S. economy produces, on average, 200,000 new jobs per month, this number is not yet an alarming one for U.S. policy makers (Leamer 2006).

Leamer is not contesting the fact that we are in the midst of a radical economic transformation, nor am I. We are indeed moving from an industrial to a postindustrial society. What is being questioned is the utility of Friedman's analysis based as it is on an awkward, misleading, and extremely confusing metaphor.

If the point of Friedman's book is that globalization is here to stay, he is probably right, but most of us undoubtedly realized this before we started reading this book. If Friedman believes that the best way to "manage" globalization is through his flat-world metaphor, he's undoubtedly wrong. No single metaphor can capture the complexity of what is happening, and it is just too simple to think otherwise.

There are so many other important ways of thinking about the world. What we really need are additional perspectives, a dialogue of competing and complementary voices, more metaphors not less, metaphors that tap into the multiple dimensions of reality, and not a single metaphor that attempts to reduce reality to just two dimensions. Friedman's book does cite numerous business leaders from around the world, friends of Thomas (FOTs), but the final product sounds more like a monologue issuing forth from a single perspective with unified economic and cultural interests than a real and substantial dialogue among people with different experiences, histories, values, hopes, and desires. It's too easy and too facile to compare different cultures to pizzas with different toppings, as Friedman does in yet another attempt to expand on his flat-world metaphor. "The flat-world platform is just like . . . pizza dough" (507), he writes. Fortunately and unfortunately, our differences (and our similarities) run much deeper than this.

If the world is not flat (or not only flat), as Friedman thinks it is, then how can we begin to get our bearings and move beyond this metaphor? Consider some additional metaphors.

The World Is Tilted

The differences between the haves and the have-nots are not getting smaller as Friedman's title might suggest, but the differences are getting bigger. Thinking of the world as tilted might be a nice starting point by reminding ourselves of all this.

Although Friedman demonstrates concern about the uneven distribution of income and wealth in the United States and around the world, it's not at all clear from Friedman's flat-world perspective *why* he should really care about this. It is not enough to think of our responsibilities to one another merely as "constraints" on our own self-interest or as some kind of "fat" purposely built into the system, as Friedman imagines it. We need deeper, more compelling metaphors than these.

The World Is Encounter

We live in a world where our deepest values are not solely about how we manipulate things, but our most important values are concerned with how we treat one another. Martin Buber talks about deepening our relationships through I–Thou encounters, a relation of subject to subject and not always subject to object. In these kinds of encounters, we treat each other as whole beings and not mere fragments. There is a profound respect for one another and not mere toleration. Buber believed that humans could approach not only other living beings in this way but inanimate objects, as well. Thinking of the world as an encounter reminds us that not only do we have much in common with one another, but there are real differences, as well.

The World Is Emergent

We must learn not only how to run faster and work harder as Friedman suggests, but we must purposely slow ourselves down, as well. We must learn how to listen to one another better and to respond more appropriately. An emergent, self-organizing world is an inherently unpredictable one. Can we learn to accept and appreciate this kind of uncertainty without *always* trying to manage it for our own purposes?

The World Is Temporal (and Spatial)

Rabbi Abraham Joshua Heschel, one of the leading Jewish theologians of the twentieth century, wrote in his slim but profound book *The Sabbath*, "Technical civilization . . . is man's triumph over space. Yet time remains impervious. We can overcome distance but can neither recapture the past nor dig out the future. Man transcends space, and time transcends man" (1951, 98).

Friedman's world is flat metaphor reminds me of Heschel's "technical civilization." The flat-world metaphor is a celebration of man's triumph (or potential triumph) over space. What is sorely missing, however, from this metaphor is an appreciation of the "sanctity" of time, as Rabbi Heschel would put it. In a flat world, there is no longer any mystery, awe, and wonder. In a flat world, everything is what it seems to be, everything is to be taken literally, at face value. In Friedman's flat deterministic landscape, freedom is merely a shadow, an illusion.

Heschel's point was *not* to denigrate our material, physical existences. His point was more subtle. "Time and space are *interrelated*," he wrote. "To overlook either of them is to be partially blind. What we plead against is man's unconditional surrender to space, his enslavement to things. We must not forget that it is not a thing that lends significance to a moment; it is the moment that lends significance to things" (1951, 6; emphasis added).

The World Is a Bridge

Rabbi Haim Nachman from Braslav, one of the greatest Hasidic masters wrote, "The whole world is a narrow bridge and the most important thing is not to fear at all." What can it mean to us to think of the world as a bridge?

Like all good metaphors, this one has many possible meanings. I would like to focus, however, on just one. Reconceiving the world as a bridge is meant to help us move beyond the philosophy of individualism on which so many of our theories depend, especially those of classical economics and its modern variants.

In the end, we don't have to be like those lions and gazelles waking up every morning, alone and frightened, and running as fast as they can. The bridge metaphor suggests that we are deeply interrelated beings. As Mikhail Bakhtin once wrote, "Consciousness is never self sufficient; it always finds itself in an intense relationship with another consciousness" (as quoted in McNamee and Gergen 1999, 11). We relate to one another, not just on a surface level, at our own convenience, but our own identities—who I am, who we are—are defined in terms of the relationships that constitute us.

The bridge metaphor shifts the focus from individual egos to the links and connections that cocreate and sustain these egos through time. There are hints of the existence of this kind of deep interrelatedness in Friedman's flat world. The reader senses Friedman's attempt to understand this when he talks, for example, about "deep collaboration" (440) at some of the world's best high-tech companies or when he talks so passionately about our need to care for and protect the environment. In the end, however, the very framework on which he operates, the flat-world platform, does not provide a sufficiently rich vocabulary and set of images to do what he and we want it to do.

CONCLUSION

The kinds of global problems we are now confronting—terrorism, global warming, environmental degradation, anti-intellectualism, the increasing gap between the rich and poor, weak and self-interested leaders, and perhaps even a diminishing appreciation for democracy itself, I believe, require not just an expanded consciousness but a change in consciousness, a consciousness willing to relax its hold on old ways of making meaning and willing to embrace a plurality of new ones.

"We have to be the masters of our imagination, not the prisoners," writes Thomas Friedman as part of his conclusion (550). I suggest that this is Friedman at his best. The question, however, is how do we do this? Do we return to old ways of thinking and just do more and more of it? Or, do we begin to experiment with new modes of dialogue, alternative stories, and multiple metaphors?

CHAPTER 8

DIALOGUE AS A RESTRAINT ON WEALTH

Technical civilization is the product of labor, of man's exertion of power for the sake of gain, for the sake of producing goods. It begins when man, dissatisfied with what is available in nature, becomes engaged in a struggle with the forces of nature in order to enhance his safety and increase his comfort. To use the language of the Bible, the task of civilization is to subdue the earth, to have dominion over the beast.

How proud we often are of our victories in the war with nature, proud of the multitude of instruments we have succeeded in inventing, of the abundance of commodities we have been able to produce. Yet our victories have come to resemble defeats. In spite of our triumphs, we have fallen victims to the work of our hands; it is as if the forces we had conquered have conquered us.

—Abraham Joshua Heschel, *The Sabbath*

I long to live a life of integrity and wholeness. As I imagine this life, it is both a life of purpose *and* comfort. It is a life where I learn to accept, appreciate, and take responsibility for the environment in which I live and of which I am a part. It is a life where I demonstrate respect and love for others through everyday actions. It demands patience and humility. I must continually learn to listen more fully, and to respond and to give back more generously. This life includes a search for a plurality of *good-enough* meanings. Where I cannot *already* find meaning, I must be prepared to create it together with others through dialogue. I must keep growing and learning even in my darkest hours, even in the face of painful suffering. This is a life where real joy and happiness are goals to be embraced and shared.

What I am describing here is a kind of spirituality, but it is not the kind of spirituality that one finds by denigrating the physical world or denying our bodies and their desires and needs.[1] In fact, from a Jewish perspective, even the so-called Evil Desire can potentially serve a legitimate moral function.[2]

From this point of view, material wealth is *a* value among many *other* values. Here is how one of the truly great Jewish theologians of the last century, Rabbi Abraham Joshua Heschel, framed it in his short but illuminating book titled *The Sabbath*: "To gain control of the world of space is certainly *one* of our tasks. The danger begins when in gaining power in the realm of space we forfeit all aspirations in the realm of time. There is a realm of time where the goal is not to have but to be, not to own but to give, not to control but to share, not to subdue but to be in accord. Life goes wrong when the control of space, the acquisition of things of space, becomes our *sole* concern" (1951, 3; emphasis added). The Sabbath and a Sabbath conscious ness, Rabbi Heschel believed, are integral to an authentic Jewish life. But the Sabbath is misunderstood if it is conceived of as a withdrawal or a moving away from the world. "Since there are so many acts which one must abstain from doing on the seventh day 'you might think I have given you the Sabbath for your displeasure; I have surely given you the Sabbath for your pleasure.' To sanctify the seventh day does not mean: Thou shalt mortify thyself, but, on the contrary: thou shalt sanctify it with all thy heart, with all thy soul and with all thy senses. 'Sanctify the Sabbath by choice meals, by beautiful garments; delight your soul with pleasure and I will reward you for this very pleasure'" (Heschel 1951, 18–19).

In Judaism, it is nearly universally recognized that wealth is one of the important ingredients that goes into living a rich and meaningful life. According to the Bible, for example, all three of the Patriarchs—Abraham, Isaac, and Jacob—were, or became, wealthy individuals possessing large numbers of cattle and herds.

"IF I AM NOT FOR MYSELF, WHO WILL BE FOR ME?"

But, once we recognize the core legitimacy of wealth to society as a human value, how do we prevent the pursuit of wealth from taking over everything else? If I like "choice meals" and "beautiful garments" so much, why should I restrict my consumption of them to just one day a week? After all, as the first century Rabbi, Hillel, once rhetorically asked, "If I am not for myself, who will be for me?"

One ancient rabbi, Shimon Bar Yochai, who lived about a hundred years after Hillel, sensed the danger, and perhaps attractions and temptations of wealth, so acutely that he and his son hid in a cave, eating nothing but the fruit from a carob tree, for more than twelve years. When they finally emerged from the cave, they immediately saw workers plowing the fields and sowing the seed. They said, "These people forsake eternal life and are engaged in temporary life!" (as quoted in Heschel, 36). Whatever they looked at was consumed by fire. A heavenly voice chastised them, though. "Have ye emerged to destroy My world? Return to your caves" (ibid).

"IF I AM *ONLY* FOR MYSELF, THEN WHAT AM I?"

Hillel and mainstream Jewish thought, unlike the cave-dwelling Rabbi Shimon Bar Yochai, recognized the significance of secular and self-interested behavior. I, too, believe that any kind of useful ethics we decide together to promote must start with an affirmation and recognition of self-interested behavior. The ethical problem is not in being self-interested, the ethical problem is in being *only* self-interested. Or, as Hillel formulated it in his second and connected rhetorical question, "If I am *only* for myself, then what am I?"

Hillel knew that we must somehow find a way to balance our own needs with the needs of others. In Jewish thought, neither *selfless* love nor *selfish* love are seen as ideals. Perhaps this is nothing more than one more restatement of the golden rule: "Love your neighbor as you love yourself" (Leviticus 19:18). But how do we operationalize this? How do we begin to enact the golden rule?

I believe, with many others, that what is being asked of us in the golden rule, and its many variants both ancient and modern, is not just a change in behavior—more of this, less of that—but a change in consciousness. We must move beyond the inherited philosophy of individualism to a new way of being in, and relating to, the world. To me, what this really means is that we must learn how to live in the moment of dialogue.

No modern Jewish thinker has done more to promote the notion of dialogue as central to Jewish ethics than Martin Buber. Throughout all of his writings, but especially in his book *I and Thou*, Buber expressed a deep and profound appreciation for interpersonal communication and human interconnectedness. As Buber stated, "God is not in me, and God is not in you, but God is what is between us." Or, on another occasion, "When two people relate to each other authentically and humanly, God is the electricity that surges between them."

Interestingly, Martin Buber (in *I and Thou*) explicitly upheld the human will to "profit and to be powerful," but he warned that these desires "have their natural and proper effect so long as they are linked with, and upheld by, his *will to enter into relation*" (emphasis added).

Buber's understanding of the central place of dialogue is well-grounded in traditional Jewish sources. For example, in Genesis, Abraham responds to God's decision to destroy Sodom by engaging God in a conversation. Abraham asks God, "Will not the judge of the whole earth act justly?" In rabbinic writings, even a cursory examination will show that dialogue among the rabbis is *the* defining characteristic of Talmudic thought and engagement. No rabbinic phrase captures this idea better than the expression "It [Jewish law and ethics] is not in heaven."

THE PURSUIT OF WEALTH AS PART OF A DIALOGUE

The pursuit, the acquisition, and the disposition of wealth are all activities that gain their ethical legitimacy as part of a larger, ongoing society-wide dialogue. To use biblical language, we can say that wealth is a necessary good when it promotes, extends, and deepens covenantal responsibilities.[3] When wealth and the power that comes with wealth, are misused to cut dialogue short, to engage in strategic communication, or to undercut democratic institutions that support open and free dialogue, wealth and power have exceeded their appropriate boundaries. In these cases, rather than enriching us, wealth impoverishes us, regardless of its "positive" effect on how we might currently measure and report gross national product. As the list of the colossal ethics failures in the last decade amply demonstrates, the unrestrained pursuit of wealth (i. e., wealth unhinged from the "will to enter into relation") has a natural tendency to colonize other human values.

In order to legitimately justify an organization's decisions and actions, corporate accountability should be, and increasingly is, viewed and described as a dialogue between the corporation and its stakeholders and not as a monologue on the part of management.[4] This means that corporate accountability requires listening to a company's diverse stakeholders as well as responding to them.

These diverse stakeholder surely must include the least well-off members of society and not just the wealthiest. "The stranger that sojourneth with you shall be unto you as the homeborn among you, and thou shalt love him as thyself; for ye were strangers in the land of Egypt" (Leviticus 19:34). But are the high aspirations set in this biblical verse really possible to achieve given the following startling statistics?

1. In the United States in 2000, income inequality was greater than at any time since the 1920s, with the richest 5 percent of all households

receiving six times more income than the poorest 20 percent of households. This statistic has risen dramatically since 1970.
2. In 2002, according to U.S. government statistics, 34.6 million people lived in poverty, about 12 percent of the total population.
3. With respect to the issue of wealth, the richest 1 percent of all households owned 42 percent of all stocks, 56 percent of all bonds, 44 percent of all trusts, 71 percent of all noncorporate businesses, and 37 percent of all nonhome real estate.

Consider, as a stark contrast to the above statistics, the ideals inherent in the Jewish institution of the Jubilee year. According to the Torah's original plan every fifty years, or about once in a lifetime, there was supposed to be a radical redistribution of wealth (Leviticus 25). While it may be hard to imagine that these laws were ever fully operative, they provide a clear statement of the Jewish pull toward economic equality and the Jewish sensitivity toward the least well-off members of society. It is impossible, of course, to derive specific policy prescriptions from these ancient laws; nevertheless, the power and attraction of the biblical worldview undercuts those contemporary conservative viewpoints that are based solely on the "sanctity of private-property."

If dialogue is going to be more than mere lip service, we must find ways not only of treating the strangers fairly, but we also must devise ways of actively seeking them out and bringing them into our houses. The following is a rabbinic *midrash* describing the difference between Job and Abraham that illustrates this point:

Now when that great calamity came upon Job, he said unto the Holy One, blessed be He: "Master of the Universe, did I not feed the hungry and give the thirsty to drink? And did I not clothe the naked?"

Nevertheless the Holy One, blessed be He, said to Job: "Job, thou has not yet reached half the measure of Abraham. Thou sittest and tarriest within thy house and the wayfarers come in to thee. To him who is accustomed to eat wheat bread, thou givest wheat bread to eat; to him who is accustomed to eat meat, thou givest meat to eat; to him who is accustomed to drink wine, thou givest wine to drink. But Abraham did not act in this way. Instead he would go forth and make the rounds everywhere, and when he found wayfarers *he brought them into his house*. To him who was unaccustomed to eat wheat bread, he gave wheat bread to eat; to him who was unaccustomed to eat meat, he gave them meat to eat; to him who was unaccustomed to drink wine, he gave wine to drink. Moreover he arose and built stately mansions on the highways and left there food and drink, and every passerby ate

and drank and blessed Heaven. (Abot de R. Natan, 7, as translated by
J. Goldin; emphasis added)

Ethics is ultimately about seeing our own humanity in the other, and
seeing the other's humanity in ourselves. On Passover, for example,
we invite the poor to join us at our *seders*. This is not just an act of
charity, this is an act of self-preservation. As Maimonides, the pre-
eminent medieval Jewish scholar, put it more than 800 years ago,
"he who locks the doors to his courtyard and eats and drinks with
his wife and family without feeding the poor and bitter of soul—his
meal is not a rejoicing in a divine commandment but a rejoicing in his
own stomach." (Twersky 1972, 108). Treating everyone with equal
human dignity may not be the sole aim of community, but it is certainly a necessary means for every other aim.

A ROLE FOR RELIGION IN BUSINESS ETHICS

Viewing the creation of wealth as part of, or as "contained by," dialogue suggests that we should view all specific prescriptions about
business ethics as, at best, incomplete, temporary, and tentative. In
my view, we don't merely inherit ethics from the past, nor do we
receive it from on high. Ethics, in my vision, is the continuous process of cocreating an emerging covenant and simultaneously promising (covenanting) to one another that we will do our best to live up
to its terms. Rabbi Jonathan Sacks, the current chief rabbi of Great
Britain, expands on this: "Covenant is the bond by which two parties
pledge themselves to one another, each respecting the freedom and
integrity of the other, agreeing to join their separate destinies into a
single journey that they will travel together, 'fearing no evil, for You
are with me'" (2005, 45).

Perhaps at the end of the day, the best gift that religion has to
offer business ethics on the topic of wealth creation is not another
list of dos and don'ts, not another code of external constraints, but
a model of how humans, ideally, could and should interact with one
another. Religion and religious discourse, based on the biblical view
that each and every one of us is "created in the image of God," might,
at its best, help us learn how to listen better, voice more honestly, and
respect one another more deeply.

Religion might remind us that carving up the world into economic,
environmental, and social domains may be useful for some purposes,
but it is ultimately as artificial as any other division. Religion might
remind us that wealth and profits are nothing more and nothing less

than human creations and that the only real and durable wealth is shared wealth. Rabbi Heschel rhetorically asked, "Is the joy of possession an antidote to the terror of time?" (p. 6). Undoubtedly not.

Maybe the hardest lesson of all that religion can teach us is to learn how to remain in the moment of dialogue, how to maintain the "will to enter into relation." We continue to speak to one another, face to face, not to forfeit wealth, not to forgo power, and not to uproot our desires. We remain in the moment of dialogue because it is here that wealth is truly enjoyed, power is legitimated, and our deepest human desires are most likely to be fulfilled. To appreciate all of this may require a change in consciousness on our part, but ultimately this mind-shift is the point of a religiously grounded business ethics.

CHAPTER 9

THE LIMITS OF DIALOGUE

That plane upon which we talk about what we think of as the orderly, accountable, self-evidently knowable and controllable characteristics of both ourselves (as autonomous individual persons) and our world, is constructed upon another, lower plane, in a set of unacknowledged and unintended, disorderly, conversational forms of interaction involving struggles between ourselves and others.

—John Shotter, *Conversational Realities*

Open, honest, inclusive, transparent, and self-reflexive dialogue is the process by which ethical norms are transmitted from one generation to the next, abandoned, replaced, criticized, improved upon, and, finally, legitimated (only to begin the process once again). This process is a most fragile one and comes with no external guarantees that it will work.

At best, dialogue produces good-enough, uncertain, temporary, and contestable outcomes dependent on the environment and the context in which ethical norms are actually realized. As Jurgen Habermas has put it, "Only those norms can claim to be valid that meet (or could meet) with the approval of all affected in their capacity *as participants in a practical discourse*" (as quoted in Unterman and Bennett 2004, 690; emphasis in original).

During the last several years, many important criticisms have been lodged against dialogue, and in this concluding chapter, it is worth looking at each of these and lingering with them for a while longer. The point is not to debate the veracity of these criticisms but to articulate them in the clearest possible way, to accept them, and to incorporate them, to the extent that it is possible, into the dialogue.

I begin by examining seven powerful criticisms of dialogue. Each of these are important in their own right, highlighting a particular weakness or blindness inherent in the very process of dialogue. These criticisms caution us to be careful in our advocacy of dialogue and to temper our optimism and enthusiasm in a realistic way.

In identifying these first seven criticisms, I am reminded of John Shotter's observation that "in our everyday social life together, we do not find it easy to relate ourselves to each other in ways which are *both* intelligible (and legitimate), *and* which also are appropriate to '*our*' (unique) circumstances." And, yet, Shotter concludes, "on occasion at least, we nonetheless do succeed in doing so" (2002, 23; emphasis in original).

These first seven criticisms are important and fundamental. But I believe each of them, in time and with patience, can become part of the very process of a self-reflexive dialogue. On occasion, these criticisms can and have been surmounted, at least for the time being. These are what I think of as "soft" criticisms, formulated not from outside of a dialogical perspective, but as part and parcel of the very process of dialogue. In this chapter, I will not attempt to resolve these criticisms, or even answer them directly, but will merely state them and let them speak for themselves. They each constitute a call for experimentation and further research on the possibilities and limits of dialogue.

In addition to these soft criticisms, the essay also identifies one last criticism that is different in kind from the earlier ones. This last criticism I label as a "hard" criticism. It is formulated not from inside of a dialogical perspective but from a stance located outside of the logic of dialogue. It is with this criticism, I believe, that we finally reach the outer limits to dialogue, where words begin to fail, speech begins to stutter, and all that remains, in spite of everything, is our desire to remain together in the space of dialogue.

SOFT CRITICISMS

Dialogues Are Never-Ending

In any real-life situation, the discursive process, the defining characteristic of dialogue, must come to an end, at least temporarily. Decisions have to be made. Actions must be taken. In practice, it is nearly impossible to attain universal agreement. And even if such agreement were claimed to have been achieved, suspicions about the legitimacy of such a dialogue would immediately be raised.

To end the process of dialogue, participants, *as a practical matter*, may agree to decision procedures like majority rule. In other circumstance, participants may choose to cede decision-making authority to experts.

But are these practical agreements to terminate the dialogue themselves universally accepted? How do these decisions' rules become legitimated if not through even more dialogue? Open-ended dialogues that lack any kind of natural mechanism of closure can thus lead to inefficient and interminable ways of organizing ourselves. This is an especially powerful criticism in times of emergency, when timely decision making is most critical for survival.

Dialogues Always Leave Out Important Stakeholders

No matter how much good faith dialogue participants bring to the table, it is inevitable that some important individuals or groups of individuals will not be present or represented. Some participants may feel that others are simply not capable of participating because of their particular status (i.e., their gender, race, religion, social class, ethnicity, sexual orientation, nationality, or age, etc.). Some participants may feel that others have not yet earned a right to participate in decision making.

Even in those circumstances where all individuals or groups who are affected by the outcomes of a dialogue are invited to participate in the dialogue, not all of them will show up or even agree to come in the first place. Stakeholders may choose to refrain from participating in a dialogue for lack of time, lack of interest, or lack of necessary skills. In other situations, stakeholders may choose not to participate in order to withhold legitimacy for fear that the invitation to participate is simply an attempt to co-opt them for purposes other than those stated explicitly.

Dialogues May Create More Dissension and Disagreement Rather Than Less

Ideally, dialogue participants listen to one another with attention and curiosity. Dialogue participants voice their own positions in a respectful and caring way. They affirm one another even if they do not always agree with each other (Gergen, McNamee, and Barrett 2001). There is an attempt to understand each other not just from our own limited and parochial points of view, but there is an attempt to imagine what the world looks like from others' viewpoints and experiences. The goal of dialogue is to enlarge our understanding by incorporating a plurality of perspectives; it is to create a shared wisdom founded on many different kinds of experiences, beliefs, and values.

This process, though, can easily breakdown. *I am* listening, *I am* being patient, tolerant, affirming, and respectful, but these *others* are loud, different, obnoxious, illogical, self-righteous, self-enclosed. *I am* here to reach understanding and to seek a deep kind of mutuality, but these *others* are here simply to rehearse old complaints and reenact old wounds.

Trust dissolves quickly, and instead of creating new forms of social capital, what little social capital we did share at the outset is dissipated and squandered in the heat of the moment. What starts out as a real attempt to achieve more and better understanding among people from different backgrounds, races, genders, and social classes ends up reinforcing and hardening old stereotypes. Dialogue can thus become unwieldy and ineffective. It can make an already tense and volatile situation even worse.

Dialogues Encourage Groupthink

More than thirty years ago, Irving L. Janis coined the term groupthink to characterize an especially negative feature of the process of decision making in highly cohesive groups. According to Janis, groupthink is "a mode of thinking that people engage in when they are deeply involved in a cohesive in-group, when concurrence-seeking becomes so dominant that it tends to override critical thinking." According to Janis then, the problem inherent in dialogue is not *too much* dissension and disagreement but *too little*. Dialogues fail because objections are not raised, and sustained critical analysis is not tolerated. Janis continued, "The term refers to a decline in mental efficiency and in the ability to test reality and to make moral judgments. Most of the main symptoms of groupthink arise because the members of decision-making groups avoid being too harsh in their judgments of their leader's or their colleagues' ideas. They adopt a soft line of criticism, even in their own thinking. At their meetings, all the members are amiable and seek complete concurrence on every important issue with no bickering or conflict to spoil the cozy atmosphere" (1971). Those dialogues in which acceptance and trust are embraced as ideal values, where listening and toleration are encouraged as essential to the process, would seem then to provide an exceptionally hospitable environment for the emergence of groupthink and its perverse consequences.

Dialogues Serve to Mask Power Rather Than Challenge It

Dialogue is promoted as a fundamental building block of democratic self-government. The health of any democracy is directly dependent on the strength, depth, complexity, and variety of those dialogues that constitute it.

Ironically, however, it has been argued that some dialogues may actually serve to weaken and undermine core democratic processes. Critics of dialogue point out an important distinction between mere conversation, on the one hand, and "democratic deliberative processes," on the other hand:

> Political deliberation entails a clear instrumental purpose, ideally remaining ever mindful of its implications beyond an individual case. Marked by disagreement—even pain—democratic deliberation contains transparent prescribed procedures governing participation and decision making so as to protect the timid or otherwise weak. In such processes, written records chronicle the interactional journey toward resolution, and in the case of writing law especially, provide accessible justification for decisions rendered. In sharp contrast, conversation is often "small talk" exchanged among family, friends, or candidates for intimacy, unbridled by set agendas, and prone to egocentric rather than altruistic goals. Subject only to unstated "rules" such as turn-taking and politeness, conversation tends to advantage the gregarious or articulate over the shy or slight of tongue. (Tonn 2005, 406–7)

Dialogue Encourages the Use of Private Forms of Communication in Public Settings

"Certain dangers lurk in employing private or social communication modes for public problem-solving" (Tonn 2005, 406). Advocates of dialogue encourage participants to consider issues from a personal point of view. They also advise examining emotions and feelings in public settings and not just facts and empirical findings. Many of the most ardent advocates of dialogue have backgrounds in psychology and family therapy. They promote "narrative and psychological approaches" in the name of "civility, cooperation, personal empowerment, and socially constructed or idiosyncratic truths" (ibid).

But is "therapeutic language" helpful in public settings? Some critics believe that it is not. Mari Boor Tonn, for example, believes that use of private forms of communication in public settings can actually work to "contain dissent, locate systemic social problems solely within individual neurosis, and otherwise fortify hegemony" (ibid).

Rather than solving problems and speaking truth to power, dialogues inspired by a therapeutic model can pollute public discussion and debate. Quoting Kenneth Burke, Tonn writes that private forms of communication—especially heartfelt confessionals—"include a kind of personal irresponsibility, as we may even relieve ourselves of private burdens by befouling the public medium" (ibid, 419).

Dialogues Solve or Attempt to Solve Problems Symbolically When in Fact These Problems Should Be Solved Through Material Means

Dialogues are designed to level the playing field. The more inclusive a dialogue is, the more apt it is to lead to acceptable outcomes. There are situations, however, where dialogue is merely symbolic.

Dialogue swims lightly on the surface and is oblivious to the deeper realities caused by the unfair allocation of economic and tangible resources in society. Dialogue tries hard to see everyone as equals, blinding itself to the harsh reality of the haves and the have-nots. While we engage in "idle" discussion, the differences between rich and poor grow wider and seemingly more permanent every day.

With regard to each of these seven criticisms identified above, the solution would seem to be more and better dialogues rather than jettisoning dialogue in favor of some other form of organizing. If it is true, as is surely the case on occasion, that "dialogue swims lightly upon the surface," the answer is to alter and deepen the dialogue rather than abandon it altogether. If, at other times, dialogue is "blinding itself to the harsh reality," dialogue itself must become more open and *seeing*, and increasingly self-conscious about its goals and effects.

Each of these criticisms demands much more attention and discussion.? One may begin to wonder, "Where are the knock-down arguments?" But this is not my purpose in this concluding chapter.

Is it possible to simply tolerate this uncertainty and ambiguity for the time being? There is a felt sense of real anxiety in identifying these criticisms and then *not* immediately countering them with more pro-dialogue arguments, with better theories, more facts, and statistically significant numbers. Maybe, though, learning to tolerate this anxiety is a good thing in itself? Perhaps the call of the hour is to patiently sharpen and deepen the criticisms still further before we attempt to resolve them once and for all?

Each of these criticisms have been formulated from inside the logic of dialogue. They do not necessarily attack the goals and the means of dialogue, but merely point out that we have not really gotten it right yet. That is why I think of these criticisms as the soft ones. These are real criticisms, but we think we know what to do with them or, at least, we think we know in which direction to proceed. In the next section, however, we turn to a different type of criticism, a criticism that does not share the goals and means of dialogue. It is a harsher and harder criticism, less friendly and more confrontational.

A Harder Kind of Criticism

Dialogues Inevitably Lead Us into the Abyss of a Hopeless Relativism—the Only Real Output of a Dialogue Is More Dialogue

This final criticism is by far the harshest and deepest critique of all. Open, honest, inclusive, transparent, and self-reflexive dialogue can not produce legitimate ethical norms; it can only produce *talk* about ethical norms.

No matter how careful we are in developing decision rules (criticism 1), no matter how many stakeholders take part in dialogue (criticism 2), no matter how much attention we place on finding just the right balance between toleration and critique (criticisms 3 and 4), no matter how much one challenges the existing power structure and is careful to cite facts and figures—and not just feelings and personal stories (criticisms 5 and 6), and no matter how much we can equalize the distribution of resources in society in a just and fair way (criticism 7), no amount of dialogue can lead us to where we really want to go. That is, dialogues—even those that produce the deepest possible interpersonal understandings and connections, even those that lead to the most profound kinds of mutuality and fellow feelings—will not yield absolute, timeless, and objective ethical principles.

This critique is different in kind from the previous ones in that it is formulated from outside the perspective of dialogue. It knows of objective and ethical principles, and it knows that these principles are derived from someplace *other than* human interactions and dialogues. These axiomatic principles precede our attempts to create them and exist independently of our acceptance of them or even our understanding of them.

This criticism does not represent a call for more and better dialogue or for more research on dialogue, but this criticism is the ultimate conversation stopper! With this criticism, we have reached the outer limits of dialogue. This is a fearful and dangerous place to be.

From the point of view of dialogue, on which all the chapters in this book are constructed, "The 'grounds' for settling arguments are to be found within arguments themselves, not outside them . . . A lack of foundations is not a lack for bases for judgment" (Shotter 2002, 48). From the point of view of this last criticism, however, this is simply not the case. In fact, quite the opposite is true.

In opening the floodgates of dialogue, one is really encouraging an anything-goes, free-for-all chaos. Perhaps John Shotter is correct when he writes, "We live our daily social lives within an ambience of conversation, discussion, argumentation, negotiation, criticism and justification; much of it to do with problems of intelligibility and the legitimation of claims to truth. Anybody wanting to deny it will immediately confront us with an empirical example of its truth. And it is this 'rooting' of all our activities in our involvements with those around us, which prevents an 'anything goes' chaos" (2002, 29). I believe he *is* right. But this "argument" works only if one is already safely inside the confines of dialogue to begin with. Outside the shared logic of dialogue, one can continue to deny Shotter's claim all he or she wants to with no accountability or responsibility to others, including Shotter, because these interpersonal entanglements are *not* the source of one's ethical principles in the first place.

With this last criticism, advocates of dialogue are pushed up against our own limits. The Other simply does not want to engage in dialogue, and there is nothing we can do to force him or her to participate. From our point of view, "Morality isn't about *forcing* people to draw certain 'rational' conclusions and then acting on them" (Johnson 1993, 258; emphasis in original). Anyone who is a teacher knows firsthand the impossibility, frustration, and deep paradox of trying to make a student engage in a dialogue against the student's own true wishes. We feel almost beaten, as if we have a gift to give to the student, but the student simply doesn't want it.

What is left for the advocates of dialogue in these kinds of situations? All we are really left with is our own *desire* to remain together in the space of dialogue. The poet Keats once wrote in a letter to his brothers that "at once it struck me what quality went to form a Man of Achievement—Negative Capability, that is, when a man is capable of being in uncertainties, mysteries, doubts without any irritable reaching after fact and reason" (as quoted in Phillips 2001, 21). This is precisely the kind of practiced attitude we need nurture when words begin to fail and dialogues are fizzling out all around us. We do so with acceptance, encouragement, patience, respect, joy, and even love. We self-consciously choose to neither surrender to our fear nor dominate our opponent.

We keep searching creatively for areas of potential agreement, and we try to finesse our differences rather than emphasize them. We believe with Seyla Benhabib that "in a world of complete interdependence among peoples and nations, in which the alternatives are between non-violent collaboration and nuclear annihilation, communicative ethics may supply our minds with just the right dose of *fantasy* such as to think beyond the old oppositions of utopia or realism, containment or conflict" (1992, 49; emphasis added).

We imagine ourselves, from time to time, adopting our opponents' point of view, living in it for a moment; we try to understand it as best we can, and yet we cannot finally accept it as our own. We sense the dialogical consciousness as a developmental accomplishment, a hard-won stage of development, and encourage others to join with us (Kegan 1982, 1994).

Ultimately, at the very limits of dialogue, all we can do is hold fast to the philosopher Alfred North Whitehead's sensible prescription. "The art of literature, vocal or written, is to adjust the language so that it embodies what it indicates" (as quoted in Jackson 1998, 160). This, at least, has been the goal of both this concluding chapter and all of the chapters included in this book.

BOTH TOGETHER AND APART: RABBI MEIR AND *AHER* (THE OTHER)

The relation to the Thou is immediate. Between I and Thou there is no terminology, no preconception and no imagination, and memory itself changes, since it plunges from singularity into the whole . . . All means are impediment. Only where all means fall to pieces, encounter happens.

—Martin Buber, *I and Thou*

It happened once that four men entered paradise, Ben Azzai, Ben Zoma, Elisha Ben Abuya, and Rabbi Akiva. Ben Azzai cast a look and died. Ben Zoma looked and became demented. Elisha Ben Abuya became an apostate. And, Rabbi Akiva, alone among the four men, entered whole and exited whole (Babylonian Talmud, Tractate Hagigah, 14b).

Because Elisha Ben Abuya became an apostate, his Talmudic colleagues refused to use his real name and referred to him, from then on, exclusively as *Aher* (literally, the Other). Using more modern terms, we might say Elisha ben Abuya was stripped of his "citizenship" among the rabbinic elite and was no longer considered a member in good standing of their Torah-centered dialogue. In the end, only one statement in all of the Mishna is attributed explicitly to this former Rabbinic giant. Elisha ben Abuya said, "If one learns when he is young, what is that like? To ink written on new paper. If one learns when he is old, what is that like? To ink written on blotted paper" (Pirkei Avot 4:25).

One might assume that Rabbi Meir, one of the greatest of all sages in the Talmudic period, and a former disciple of Elisha ben Abuya, would have immediately terminated his friendship with *Aher*. This is *not* how the Talmudic story proceeds, however. In fact, the Talmud records for posterity several poignant conversations between Rabbi Meir and *Aher*.

In one enigmatic episode, *after* his apostasy, *Aher* is heard asking Rabbi Meir a question about the correct reading of a verse from *Kohelet* (Ecclesiastes). *Aher* asks, "What is the meaning of the biblical verse, 'God has made even the one as well as the other?'" Rabbi Meir answers him, "It means that for everything God created, He also created its counterpart. He created mountains and created hills; He created seas, and created rivers." In turn, *Aher* responds back to Rabbi Meir, "Your master Rabbi Akiva did not explain it in this way. Rabbi Akiva said 'He created righteous and he created wicked; He created the Garden of Eden and created Gehinnom'" (Babylonian Talmud, Tractate Hagigah, 15a).

This episode raises more questions than it answers. Why is an avowed apostate asking questions about the correct reading of a Torah text in the first place? Why is Rabbi Meir bothering to answer him at all? What is the significance of the text *Aher* chooses to ask about? What is the significance of Rabbi Meir's answer to him? Finally, why is *Aher* citing Rabbi Meir's teacher Rabbi Akiva and pointing out the differences between their two answers?

It is beyond the scope of this chapter to answer these questions in any detail, but what is obvious in this story is that even when the dialogue stops, the personal relationships don't have to. Even when our shared assumptions about the world and how it works are so different and so exotic to one another and real dialogue has become impossible, the conversations do not have to stop altogether.

Both Rabbi Meir's behavior and his interpretation to the verse in *Kohelet* suggests, among other things, that even the Other is not quite so other after all. Our differences do not make us into exact opposites (as perhaps Rabbi Akiva maintains), but our differences are more like those between mountains and hills, or seas and rivers. Different, yes, but still in many fundamental ways the same.

Both Rabbi Meir and *Aher*, former teacher and former disciple, demonstrate a rare ability to remain in the space of dialogue even while they are separated by an abyss of silence. No words can possibly bridge their different worldviews. And, yet, there they remain—both together *and* apart—forever on the pages of the Talmud.

On another occasion, the Talmud relates the story of *Aher* and Rabbi Meir going out together on the Sabbath. *Aher* is riding a horse, a forbidden act on the Sabbath, and Rabbi Meir, remarkably, is walking along behind him "to learn Torah at his mouth." Suddenly, *Aher* stops in the middle of the conversation and says, "Meir, turn back for I have already measured by the paces of my horse that thus far extends the Sabbath limit." Rabbi Meir replies, "Thou, too, go back!" *Aher* responds that it is now too late for him to return for he has heard from "behind the veil—Return you backsliding children—except *Aher*" (Babylonian Talmud, Tractate Hagigah, 15a).

This story is more difficult and complex than the first one. It appears now that Rabbi Meir not only continues to discuss matters of Torah with *Aher*, but he also returns to his former status of disciple. How can this be? Has not *Aher* forfeited his authority in sacred matters? How is it that *Aher*, who lost his way in paradise, might still have something to teach Rabbi Meir?

Most unfathomable of all in this story is that it is *Aher*—the Other—who must tell Rabbi Meir not to cross over the Sabbath boundary. *Aher*, and not Rabbi Meir, is the one who has been counting their steps and measuring the distance that they have traveled together from home. Why is it that *Aher* even cares about the Sabbath boundary? After all, from his own perspective, this boundary is merely an imaginary one with no real significance whatsoever. It is only from Rabbi Meir's point of view that this line is meaningful.

This story begins by telling us that Rabbi Meir follows *Aher* out on the Sabbath day to "learn Torah at his mouth." It is fair to ask then, what possible Torah lesson does Rabbi Meir learn from this episode? And, what lesson does the reader of this story learn from the Other? Finally, and most provocative of all, are there lessons that we can *only* learn from the Other?

Although there is a tragic note to this story, "Return you backsliding children—except *Aher*," I think that it is also a profoundly hopeful and optimistic one. Elisha Ben Abuya and Rabbi Meir are both demonstrating to us across the ages that *it is* possible to care deeply about one another even when profound existential differences divide us. Elisha Ben Abuya has been banished from the dialogue. He is one of Judaism's most famous apostates, and yet without him, Rabbi Meir, one of the greatest of all Talmudic scholars, would have continued on beyond the Sabbath limit.

Martin Buber reminds us that sometimes it is despite our best efforts, despite our clever and well thought-out plans, that "encounter happens." "The relation to the Thou is immediate," he promises.

Perhaps, then,

> it is precisely when we
> reach the outer limits of dialogue,
> are faced with an Other so strange and so different from ourselves,
> stop trying so damn hard, and
> stop holding on to our old selves so tightly,
> that a whole new order of dialogue can emerge.
> After all, "encounter happens."

Appendix

An Invitation to Dialogue

The suffering of adult faith is located in learning how to hold on to, and when to let go of, the perceptions, patterns, and relationships that one experiences as partaking in ultimate value and truth. The journey through shipwreck, gladness, and amazement can have particular power in adult lives, and it can be recognized as one way of describing the deep process by which we become at home in the universe.

To be at home is to be able to make meaning of one's own life and of one's surroundings in a manner that holds, regardless of what may happen at the level of immediate events. To be deeply at home in this world is to dwell in a worthy faith.

—Sharon Daloz Parks, *Big Questions, Worthy Dreams*

Dear Students:

As we begin a new semester, it's helpful to explain some of my thoughts about why I teach business ethics. This letter is an attempt to share my hopes and concerns for the new school year. As your teacher, I possess a degree of power over you. You have a right to know how I plan to use this power.

Let me begin with a broad statement of purpose. After several years of teaching this course and experimenting, I have settled on the following overall educational goal: As a teacher, I strive to encourage and facilitate *ethical dialogues* among students and myself. I think of myself not only as a host, someone who is already participating in these ethical dialogues, but also as someone who is inviting students into the party. So, let me pause for a brief moment and say to you, "Welcome to the big leagues, my friend."

The goal is to create with the class an environment in which you, the student, can develop the capacities to engage in ethical dialogues as full participants, and ultimately not just as participants-in-training. When students become ethics teachers and teachers become ethics students, the activity of teaching has been successful.

My ultimate goal as your teacher is to use my own power to empower you in the classroom and beyond. But what does this mean in practical, everyday terms? In the coming months, we will try to create a space between us, a space where we can play with deeply serious ideas together; a comfortable, nonconfrontational, and nonthreatening place where we can begin to engage in ethical dialogues—right here and right now.

This is a place where we can mutually recognize each other as unique and special people *and* as equally important and valuable human beings who share an ability to think, feel, reason, act, and grow together. The goal of a good dialogue is to be able to work together to create a complex mosaic that none of us can produce alone.

Ethics is not about me and it's not about you; it is about you and me agreeing on what we feel comfortable doing to and with each other. I call this shared agreement, in more formal terms, a covenant.

In my view, we don't merely inherit ethics from the past, nor do we receive it from on high. Ethics, in my vision, is the continuous process of cocreating this emerging covenant and simultaneously promising (covenanting) to one another that we will do our best to live up to its terms. I like to imagine us just sitting around a dining room table and engaging in frank and animated conversation, each of us taking turns contributing to the flow of the dialogue and learning important things about ourselves and each other from it.

In order to participate in this process and learn ethics, we will need to learn and practice listening, voicing, and respecting.

Learning to Listen

To actively participate in this new kind of space, students must become acquainted with the moral vocabulary already in use and the ethical discussions that are already taking place. To learn the language competently, one must listen to it being spoken and read it voraciously. All the while, we begin to experiment with it playfully. What happens when I say such and such? What kind of reaction do I get from you?

Before you formulate an opinion about something, about anything at all, you've got to know what the subject is. Otherwise, you're just relying on some authority figure you may or may not even be aware of. What is it that people are already talking about when they claim to be talking about ethics? Are they talking about universal rules of conduct that have always been true and always will be true? Are they talking about identity? (What kind of a person am I?) Are they talking about power? (How do I get you to do what I want you to do?) Or are they talking about all of these things bunched together at once?

The first step is one of discovery for you. These ethical dialogues *are already* taking place out there in the world. They are embedded in literature, film, philosophy, education, religion, psychoanalysis, science, the social sciences, art, and even in our casual and everyday doings and conversations. The contents of these dialogues are as varied as the participants. The subjects include technology, business, medicine, separation of church and state, and democracy. We ask ourselves, using the language and vocabulary of the various disciplines, what obligations do we owe to one another? How transparent must I or we be? What rights do we possess? Who are the legitimate authorities, and on what basis do they gain their legitimacy?

To begin, you must turn down your own thoughts and immerse yourself in these dialogues. Open yourself up. Be curious about them. Wonder about them. Be affected by them. Hear them. Accept them for what they are. Surrender to them. Imagine why so many people are so deeply invested in them. Care about them. Who says what, and why?

As strange as it sounds, listening is a complex and excruciatingly subtle task, and its very meaning expands as you grow older. We learn and relearn how to listen and accept each other only with great fear and trepidation. This process is infinitely more difficult than simply debating an opponent with the hope of scoring points against him.

You may begin to wonder suddenly, if I open myself up to you and all of your foreign ideas, where is the guarantee that you won't overwhelm me, hurt me, and, worst-case scenario, eradicate me (if only with your words)? Maybe you're just trying to have fun at my expense. Who knows?

One of the scariest things of all is to find out that I can provide no perfect guarantee to you that I will not hurt you. And yet, it is almost universally accepted that one must trust his or her teacher in order to learn. The truth is that you can never be certain about me, nor should you even strive for such certainty. So learn to trust carefully.

In reality, perfect certainty is a myth, and always a debilitating one. The best you can hope for, in an imperfect world like this one, is my promise to you that I'm trying my best to help you to learn and grow as a person. But notice, here, that once we're talking about promises, we're already doing ethics together.

For students and for all of us, learning to listen in a dangerous world is really never-ending. How many times do I think to myself when I'm reading, listening to people talk, or hearing a student's complaint, "I'm missing something here. Something big." So before I go to the next step, I just want to alert you to be prepared to keep looping back to this one. "This is what I thought we were talking about, but as I listen to you more carefully, I guess not. I think I'm hearing you, but it's just my own voice, disguising itself as yours, and fooling me again."

LEARNING TO VOICE

Despite all this uncertainty and precisely because of it, to participate in ethical dialogues as equal partners in a world where power is unevenly distributed, we must learn how to respond to one another even though we can never be sure that we understand each other.

To engage in ethical dialogues as full participants, students must learn how to voice their own opinions and their own ideas. This requires listening to the other, but it requires listening to oneself, as well. What do *I* think about this issue and why? What are *my* beliefs and desires and where did they come from?

Ralph Waldo Emerson in his famous essay "Self-Reliance" once wrote, "A man should learn to detect and watch that gleam of light which flashes across his mind from within more than the lustre of the firmament of bards and sages. Yet he dismisses without notice his own thought, because it is his. In every work of genius we recognize our own rejected thoughts: they come back to us with a certain alienated majesty" (As quoted in Isaacs, William, *Dialogue and the Art of Thinking Together*, 163). But just as there exists a fear in listening to you, there is fear, and for some like me, an even greater fear, in voicing. What's worse than not understanding you is learning that I don't even understand myself. As I voice my own opinions and subject them to your approval or disapproval, I realize how tentative my own views are. "I think this is what I believe, but to tell you the truth, I'm not so sure now. So, after all, who am I?"

How can a teacher help students overcome this fear? Perhaps the best way is by simply modeling this behavior. As teachers, we strive to voice our own beliefs with clarity, conciseness, and conviction. We must take responsibility for our ideas, and we must hold ourselves accountable to our students. I believe this to be true because x, y, and z are probably true. If I find out that x, y, and z may not be the case after all, I pledge to reexamine my belief, give it up, and start again, if necessary, or, at least, hold my belief more lightly.

As we engage in ethical dialogues, we must also be prepared to state flatly, "I just don't know" or harder yet, "I thought I knew, but

I guess I really don't." In fact, as I get older, I attempt to hold fewer and fewer beliefs about the world. Paraphrasing William James, we should only believe precisely what we really need to believe to grow and to thrive together in this world and no more.

LEARNING TO RESPECT

Ethical dialogues—listening to one another and voicing our hopes and beliefs about the emerging covenant—are achievable only in an atmosphere of respect. If you cannot respect me or I cannot respect you, I cannot possibly hope to teach you. I must ask you, What is in play, and what is out of bounds? And, I must respect your answers. So, too, you must ask me, What are the rules of this classroom? What is considered acceptable and what is considered unacceptable behavior here? And you, too, must respect my answers.

Respect includes coming to class on time with assignments completed. Respect includes refraining from mocking and teasing one another and refraining from yelling at one another. Respect means that I, too, must come to class on time, prepared, and organized. Fundamentally, respect includes establishing boundaries and living within them.

Paradoxically, respect also implies an openness to one another. The only way one can participate in the kind of ethical dialogues that I'm talking about here is if each of us pledges that our own beliefs, desires, and actions are fallible and subject to change, growth, and development. I must be willing to tolerate deep change in response to your revelations. Not one of my beliefs should hold me hostage. Ethical dialogues are different than normal discussion and debates. In a debate, my goal is to get you to accept my beliefs. In a dialogue, I participate in order to teach and to be taught. I participate to voice and to listen. One sign that we are really participating in dialogue is if I suddenly take up defending your position and you suddenly take up mine. Neither one of us is fully committed to his or her own opinion. Here's a simple formula: No openness—no respect—no ethical dialogues.

These are my aspirations. I want to use whatever power I do have as a teacher to create with you a learning environment where we can begin to talk to one another as equals. I want to learn to trust you as I want you to learn to trust me. I want to motivate you and excite you about ethics and, in particular, business ethics. I want to demonstrate to you the fundamental importance of ethics to our lives. I want you to think of ethics as something real and tangible, as something alive, engaging, and responsive.

Jacob's Experience

These are, of course, high aspirations. Just how high and fragile these aspirations are came home to me a couple of years ago as I read Jacob's (not his real name) final paper.

Jacob is a bright, serious, ambitious, and highly articulate young man. When he wrote his paper, he was a senior, looking forward to attending a prestigious law school in just six months time. He began his paper by noting, "I took the class because of my interest in the subject; the majority of the students took the class to fulfill a requirement to graduate, however I already had fulfilled the requirement and took the course primarily out of intellectual desire" (Please note: all quotes are real and exact.) "Great!" I thought to myself, "this is exactly the kind of students who can benefit most from my style of inclusive teaching and class discussions."

Unfortunately, as he continued to tell his story, it turns out that he had an extremely hard time in my class. In his paper, he communicated his feelings and frustrations to me. He stated plainly that "college [is] a place that purportedly facilitates intellectual honesty and growth, although as I found out, [it] can easily stunt and even retard those ambitions." He continued,

> I felt extremely shortchanged in my experience in the class. Much to my consternation, loud students dominated the course, consistently shouting over my attempts to participate in the one-sided class discussions. Apparently the students' antics were so prevailing, that the professor never could turn his attention to the remainder of the class, the section of more reserved students that could have been identified by my outstretched hand and normally-toned voice emanating from its midst. Consequently, my attempt to discuss the professor's arguments and my routine yearning for clarification of those arguments, almost always went unrealized and unfulfilled. It was clear the professor was aware of the problem, as he often rebuked students in the class for their conduct, yet nothing was done to rectify what became a waste of many students' resources and time. Students like myself became frustrated and disillusioned.

To tell you the truth, these remarks stung me deeply and felt almost like a slap in the face, a deep rebuke. Jacob was attacking my competence as a teacher. In the paper, he reassured me that he did not want to offend me, hurt my feelings, or to be "misconstrued as a disrespectful person—results that I surely regard as wrongs due to my conviction in the maxim 'love thy neighbor as thyself.'" But I guess while these words were written to soothe me, their real effect was to magnify my anger and feed my feelings of inadequacy. In the very same paragraph in which Jacob pledged his allegiance to loving his neighbor, he also reminded me and himself that "Should I do poorly on the paper, I would risk devastating the fragile average that I was nursing in the class up to that point—a scenario that could produce a 'C' or worse on my final transcript."

It was hard to read these descriptions of my class and listen to what Jacob was saying, especially when the memories were still so fresh in my mind. Maybe Jacob was right. Maybe the class discussions that I had taken such pride in were uneven and unfair. For sure, Jacob was correct when he noted that I had often (too often) rebuked students in the class for their inappropriate conduct. "But, whose fault was that?" I blithely reassured myself. I also triumphantly wondered "Where was Jacob when I needed him most?"

Looking back, now, two years later, I begin to see some of the irony in Jacob's paper and my own responses. Jacob and I both want the same things. We both want college to be a place that facilitates intellectual honesty and growth. And, we both want it to be a place where ethical dialogues can flourish and multiply. And, to be perfectly honest, we had both been disappointed with what had actually transpired during the semester (that's exactly why his paper hurt so much). The class had hardly been a total success, even in my view. But, ironically, even with all of the problems in my classroom, here was Jacob emerging and voicing his beliefs with "clarity, conciseness, and conviction," which is exactly what I want from all of my students. With 20/20 hindsight, I can begin to respect Jacob's point of view and to admire his courage in openly stating his convictions and daringly criticizing my teaching on his final paper.

When I was trying to encourage students to formulate their own opinions and to learn how to defend them in a reasonable way, Jacob heard me as demanding him to "robotically" spit "back the beliefs of the class's founder and professor in the course's final assignment." When Jacob was trying to write a paper in which he would voice his "personal views and critique the course's substance and procedure," I heard him as whining and missing the whole point of the course!

This breakdown in communication was especially true in his second critique. Here's Jacob's second point in his own words:

> Just as tragic [as the one-sided class discussions] was an idea conveyed as part of the course's curriculum, which I felt was not only intellectually unsound, but also incredibly dangerous. As part of the professor's closing

segment of the course, he conveyed that it is good to find a compromise between one's aspirations and one's values. But what bothered me (and still does) is that this "sidestepping" philosophy is devoid of the notion of wrong and right, and instead only employs the notion of subjective good and bad (i.e., only relies on one's conscience). For example, the evaluative mechanism at every step of the professor's approach involved subjectivity. "How do my feelings . . . define, for me, the right versus right conflict? How deep are the moral roots . . . which values and commitments [do I] really have . . . ? Which of my abiding instincts and commitments . . . [will I] struggle to reshape?" (Badarcacco, 71–76, [as quoted by Jacob]). The underlying flaw is that sometimes, the conscience can suggest an evil approach; if one was raised in an evil community, one's "moral identity" might actually be quite immoral, and would result in people making immoral decisions. Thus, the outcome of the professor-sanctioned views is the facilitation of falsehood and the subsequent loss of productive individuals in life's ultimate purpose, perceiving the truth of our existence.

Jacob's critique has several parts to it, and I would like to untangle them as best as I can. Jacob states that the curriculum is "intellectually unsound" and "incredibly dangerous." He describes my advocacy of compromise as "sidestepping" and "devoid of the notion of right and wrong." He cites Joseph Badaracco's questions contained in his book *Defining Moments*—a required text for the course—as Exhibit A in his indictment. He notes the "underlying flaw" in Badaracco's (and by extension, my approach) is that "sometimes, the conscience can suggest an evil approach." The upshot of all of this is the "facilitation of falsehood and subsequent loss of productive individuals in life's ultimate purpose." What is life's ultimate purpose according to Jacob? "Perceiving the truth of our existence."

As with Jacob's first critique, my initial response was to shut down and protect my own fragile ego. Intellectually unsound? Incredibly dangerous? Sidestepping? Devoid of the notion of right and wrong? Facilitation of falsehood? These are tough accusations to listen to and absorb. And, to make matters even worse, just a few paragraphs later, Jacob added with a flourish, "The bottom line was that I felt forced into accepting the professor's approach by being assigned a final paper demanding me to think in a way that I had not yet accepted to be true. Not only is this 'collegiate blackmail" unethical, but me misrepresenting my beliefs would be no shining act of morality."

In listening to Jacob and taking his critique seriously, one of the questions that I am faced with is how did things go so wrong between us? In a class that was designed to facilitate ethical dialogues, in a class where I tried in a very self-conscious way to encourage listening, voicing, and respecting, Jacob accuses me of engaging in the unethical activity of "collegiate blackmail." I wanted the class to be a nonconfrontational space between us, a place where Jacob would feel comfortable to examine his own beliefs and to participate, as an equal partner, in dialogue.

I view this invitation to Jacob and all of his classmates as an unmitigated good, and that's why I'm so shocked by Jacob's response. In my mind I'm handing over a gift to Jacob, and in his mind he is imagining me as taking something away from him that he cherishes deeply.

What I find so confusing about Jacob's paper is that he begins it with a critique about not having ample opportunity to take part in the class dialogues. This suggests to me that he views dialogue as a *good* thing. He even states explicitly at one point that the give and take of dialogue could have "been a source of growth resulting from comparing and contrasting of ideas and utilizing my mind in philosophical scrutiny." The problem here, as I hear it, was not with the quality of the gift that I wanted to hand over, but it was that in my inability to control the class I simply didn't give it to him.

In his second critique, however, he begins to question whether or not the gift of listening, voicing, and respecting is really such a good thing after all. And, in fact, he concludes that it is not! When Jacob points out that one might have been brought up in an "evil community" and therefore one's "moral identity" might be "quite immoral," he is reflecting not just a deep fear of the other but a profound fear of his own character. Why engage in dialogue when both your moral identity and mine might be quite immoral? What good are good intentions when we both might be evil?

Jacob enters my class, presumably, "perceiving the truth of our existence," and he wants to make sure that he leaves the class fully intact, "upholding his convictions when it comes to matters of truth, a widespread ideal posed by Rabbis and philosophers alike."

I was looking for a rigorous and logical consistency from Jacob, and when I didn't find it in his paper, Jacob's grade suffered. Jacob was looking for an authority figure to dispense the truth of our existence, and when I refused to give this to him, he viewed my demand for dialogue as coercive (collegiate blackmail).

I believe that there are many lessons to be gleaned from Jacob's experiences, but the one that I would like to emphasize here is the need in learning about ethics to keep returning to the space of dialogue. This is not an easy task.

It's hard to stand inside and listen to how one's most cherished beliefs sound to someone else. It's hard to voice one's own opinions and to know that one's voice will probably be misunderstood and may even prove to be hurtful. It's hard to respect the other and to stay open to their critiques even when you think they're flat-out wrong, or worse yet, trying to hurt you. It's hard to respect the other when you can't even trust your own good intentions (maybe you and I were brought up in evil communities).

From my own point of view, I don't agree with Jacob's judgment that my curriculum was somehow unethical, but I do appreciate his frustration with my "sidestepping" and his sense of the "incredible" danger inherent in engaging in dialogue.

Jacob concludes his paper by stating that "What is clear is that I cannot base my life on feelings of anxiety and temporal security. I know that upholding ideals such as honesty and the pursuit of wisdom will bring a person to true happiness."

Here's my problem with Jacob's formulation. In opting out of the dialogue, I *can* reduce my own anxiety. I am certain that I'm right but only because there is no one else left to challenge me. The downside of this solution is that once I recognize the true cost of such existential isolation, I can no longer tolerate it or believe in it.

Rather than following our instinct to turn away from the other(s) and flee, like the great biblical prophet Jonah, we must learn to turn toward and confront the other no matter how deserving of punishment or illogical we may think he or she is. Instead of denying the anxiety of discovering that one lives in an ambiguous, inconsistent, uncertain, and often inhospitable world, let's invite each other in to talk about what we can do about it. My own conception of the "truth of our existence" will always, at best, be partial and plausible rather than total and certain. It will always be growing and developing rather than final and complete. It will always be a function of the quality of our dialogues and not dependent solely on my own genius and ingenuity.

In the end, I don't think Jacob is so much different than any of my other students, perhaps he's just more articulate. He wants desperately to have his fair chance to participate in an open and unencumbered dialogue. He knows it to be a "source of growth resulting from comparing and contrasting of ideas and utilizing my mind in philosophical scrutiny." He also knows that such participation when done with integrity and seriousness is dangerous and full of anxiety. It can be a place that can "easily stunt and even retard those ambitions."

What if it turns out that when it comes to ethics there are no "experts" to tell us what to do? From Jacob's current perspective, this is an intolerable and unacceptable conclusion. Winston Churchill once said that democracy is the worst form of government, except for all the others. I think there is something similar to be said about dialogue in the classroom. It is the worst form of teaching, except for all the others.

Jacob's paper, rather than indicating the impossibility of teaching ethics through dialogue, shows how slow and messy it all is. There is no preexisting bridge between student and student or between students and teacher. In ethical dialogues, we are building the bridge together as we walk on it. This means that teachers must learn to accept, appreciate, and build on students' inconsistencies and that students must learn to trust a teacher who claims, somewhat oddly in our culture, that he is expending his own power in order to empower them.

How Did Things Go So Wrong Between Us?

Maybe the whole point is that as long as Jacob and I can keep the dialogue going, things haven't really gone so wrong between us. My desire for a different kind of paper from Jacob is my problem and not his. Jacob was hardly trying to stop the dialogue. Tellingly, even as Jacob was accusing me of collegiate blackmail, he still kept open the possibility that I was right. "I felt forced into accepting the professor's approach by being assigned a final paper demanding me to think in a way that *I had not yet accepted to be true*" (emphasis added). This last phrase, in my reading, signals an openness and tolerance on Jacob's part for growth and development that his harsh criticism almost hides. In addition, he states explicitly that "writing this paper was one of the hardest things I have ever done. I am very uncomfortable with the thought of offending you or even the *possibility of discouraging you from teaching such a critical course*" (emphasis added).

I can assure Jacob that his paper has not discouraged me from teaching this course again, but quite to the contrary, this paper has helped me to improve my teaching and has helped me to think through how to be a more hospitable host in the future. It has given me a deeper appreciation for the difficulties that students face in my class, and it has encouraged me to be more tolerant of what I view as students' complexities and inconsistencies. At the same time, I would like to imagine that Jacob, with time, has come to the recognize (contrary to his protestations) that he, too, grew from our experiences together, even if I did not give him exactly what he had wanted from me. In giving you students exactly what you expect from me, am I really giving you anything of lasting value at all?

Big Questions

Certainty may be impossible, but we still make choices that have consequences for ourselves and those we love. Particularly in relation to important life choices, a person may begin to look for a place to stand, a way of dwelling viably in an uncertain world. He or she may begin to value those ways of composing truth and making moral choices that are more adequate than other options. This is a search for a place of commitment within relativism.

The formation of commitment in a relativized world requires taking self-conscious responsibility for one's own thinking and knowing. Now one becomes conscious of joining other adults in discerning what is adequate, worthy, and valuable, while remaining aware of the finite nature of all judgments.

—Sharon Daloz Parks, *Big Questions, Worthy Dreams*

In learning ethics, business or otherwise, we begin to examine life's big questions. How should I behave in this particular situation? What are my responsibilities to the various communities to which I belong? Is the sole goal of business to maximize profits? What should I believe in? Is there a transcendent reality? Are my own desires legitimate or should I attempt to uproot or sublimate them? Does anything I do, think, or say really make a difference? If so, to whom? What do I stand for? What is it that makes me the same person over time? What does it mean for a person to grow and develop? How can I learn to accept what I cannot change and how can I learn to tolerate difference? Who are the appropriate authorities? How I do I balance my own needs against the needs of other people?

Raising these questions and trying to answer them adequately makes us feel vulnerable. We cling to our old beliefs like we might cling to a buoy in a storm, imagining that if we hold onto the buoy more lightly we will be drowned in the ocean. But perhaps beliefs are less like buoys in a storm and more like sailboats on a windy day. In letting out the sail just a bit we may catch the wind that will take us where we want to go, out to sea or safely back to shore.

Is there anyway to avoid what Sharon Daloz Parks describes as "taking self-conscious responsibility for one's own thinking and knowing?" The ultimate lesson I glean from Jacob's paper is that once the genie of "taking self-conscious responsibility" has been let out of the bottle, it is impossible to put back in. At the same time that Jacob is criticizing my class as intellectually unsound, incredibly dangerous, sidestepping, devoid of the notion of right and wrong, and facilitating falsehoods, he is also voicing and explaining his own views. Presumably, Jacob expects me to listen with openness and respect to his critique, just as I hope that he listens and respects my views. As this process of dialogue unfolds, we begin to recognize what it is that we are already doing together. We are slowly and painstakingly becoming conscious of the fact that we are "joining other adults in discerning what is adequate, worthy, and valuable, while remaining aware of the finite nature of all judgments."

From Jacob I have learned that this is a *most gradual* process. It's possible to hold two sets of seemingly contradictory beliefs at the same time even if my theory doesn't allow for this. It is possible to take self-conscious responsibility for one's own thinking and at the same time continue to look to our "rabbis and philosophers" to simply tell us what is "true" and what is "false."

We constantly move back and forth from one way of making meaning to another more comfortable way. Jacob's paper is useful and important to me because he is reminding me about how complex real human beings are. I often fall into the trap of wanting my students to conform to my preexisting theories. I don't like surprises anymore than Jacob does. I sometimes *do* want everyone to think like me, to act like me, and to value what I value. And, so, although Jacob and I are very different human beings, we are also remarkably similar in so many ways.

As your teacher, this semester, I have a responsibility to maintain the space of dialogue between us. I am your host inviting you to participate in the process of ethical dialogues. I believe with the master educator Robert Kegan that "Meaning is, in its origins, a physical activity (grasping, seeing), a social activity (it requires another), a survival activity (in doing it, we live). Meaning is the primary human motion, irreducible. It cannot be divorced from the body, from social experience, or from the very survival of the organism. Meaning depends on someone who recognizes you. Not meaning by definition, is utterly lonely. Well-fed warm, and free of disease, you may still perish if you cannot 'mean.' . . . Who comes into a person's life may be the single greatest factor of influence to what that life becomes" (Kegan 1982, 19).

It is my intention to both recognize and accept you as you are even as I challenge you to think more carefully and more critically than ever before. I will introduce some of my beliefs and values into our conversations as the semester progresses, but my intention is not to indoctrinate you into a set of beliefs but to make you more self-reliant *and* more comfortable in recognizing just how much we each truly depend on one another.

Let me conclude with a quote from one of the most outstanding philosophers and educators of the twentieth century, John Dewey: "An undesirable society is one which internally and externally sets up barriers to free intercourse and communication of experience. A society which makes provision for participation in its good of all its members on equal terms and which secures flexible readjustment of its institutions through interaction of the different forms of associated life is in so far democratic. Such a society must have a type of education which gives individuals a personal interest in social relationships and control, and the habits of mind which secure social changes without introducing disorder" (*Democracy and Education*, 99).

It is to this vision that I pledge allegiance.

NOTES

CHAPTER 3

1. During much of the twentieth century, Rabbi Soloveitchik, also known as the Rav, was the unquestioned leader of modern Orthodox Judaism. He served as *Rosh Yeshiva* of the Rabbi Isaac Elchanan Theological Seminary of Yeshiva University.
2. See Rabbi Soloveitchik's discussion concerning Naamah, the sister of Tubal-Cain. He writes, "Beauty, uncouth and unrefined but irresistible, seducing man and contributing to his downfall, emerges in the Biblical arena for the first time—according to the midrash . . . in the person of Naamah." He continues that she is the "incarnation of unhallowed beauty" and is "not so much an individual as an idea, not only a real person but a symbol of unredeemed beauty."
3. For a formal discussion on this topic see Robert Kegan's *The Evolving Self* (1982) and *In Over our Heads* (1994).

CHAPTER 5

1. There is a hint of this idea in the traditional Talmudic view that when Israel performs commandments, the two cherubim situated in the holy of holies turn toward one another, and when Israel sins, the cherubim turn away. The rabbis held an even bolder conception that when Israel made the pilgrimage to the Temple in Jerusalem, the priests would remove the curtain separating them from the holy of holies "and show them the cherubim that were intertwined with one another, and say to them: 'Behold! Your love [hibbah] before God is like the love of the male and female'" (Idel 2005, 31).

CHAPTER 8

1. I agree wholeheartedly with Georges Enderle when he writes, "If the material world is considered inferior or even evil and if hostility towards the human body prevails, wealth cannot but share these qualities and is likely to be denigrated" (2007).
2. "And God saw all that He had made, and found it *very* good. And there was evening, and there was morning, the sixth day" (Genesis 1:31; emphasis added). Commenting on this biblical verse, the rabbis asked why the text included the seemingly extraneous word "very"? How does this word add to the meaning of this statement, as it must? Here is how they answered

this question: "Rabbi Nahman said in Rabbi Samuel's name: 'Behold, it was good' refers to the Good Desire; 'And behold, it was very good' refers to the Evil Desire. Can then the Evil Desire be very good? That would be extraordinary! But without the Evil Desire, however, no man would build a house, take a wife, and beget children." This is an extraordinary idea, and it is fundamental to my understanding of what it means to live a life of integrity and wholeness. According to the ancient rabbis, *everything* comes from God and is therefore good. The Evil Desire is so called because of its destructive potential, but at the same time, the need for desire and its positive overtones are emphasized.

3. In Chapter 1, I defined covenant as a voluntary agreement among independent but equal agents to create a "shared community." This primary purpose of the agreement is to consciously provide a stable social location for the interpretation of life's meanings in order to help foster human growth, development, and the satisfaction of legitimate human needs (see also Pava 2003, 2).

4. The Global Reporting Initiative is perhaps the single best example of this.

BIBLIOGRAPHY

Aronica, Ronald, and Mtetwa Ramdoo. *The World Is Flat? A Critical Analysis of Thomas L. Friedman's New York Times Bestseller.* Tampa: Meghan-Kiffer Press, 2006.

Badaracco, Joseph. *Defining Moments.* Boston: Harvard Business School Press, 1997.

———. *Leading Quietly.* Boston: Harvard Business School Press, 2002.

Benhabib, Seyla. *Situating the Self: Gender, Community and Postmodernism in Contemporary Ethics.* New York: Routledge, 1992.

Benjamin, Jessica. "From Many into One: Attention, Energy and the Containing of Multitudes," *Psychoanalytic Dialogues* 15, no. 2 (2005): 185–202.

Berman, Saul. "Modern Orthodoxy: In Quest of Holiness." Keynoted speech, Edah Conference, New York City, February 14–15, 1999.

Bohm, David *On Dialogue,* London and New York: Routledge, 1996.

Briskin, Alan. *The Stirring of Soul in the Workplace.* San Francisco: Berrett-Koehler, 1998.

Brown, Juanita, with David Isaacs. *The World Café: Shaping Our Futures Through Conversations That Matter.* San Francisco: Berrett-Koehler, 2005.

Broyde, Michael, and Steven Resnicoff. "The Corporate Veil and Halakhah." In *Jewish Business Ethics: The Firm and Its Stakeholders,* edited by Aaron Levine and Moses Pava, 272 Northvale, NJ: Jason Aronson, 1999.

Buber, Martin, *I and Thou.* New York: MacMillan, 1958.

Buchholz, R., and Rosenthal, S. *Rethinking Business Ethics: A Pragmatic Approach.* Oxford: Oxford University Press, 2000.

Butler, Judith. *Giving an Account of Oneself.* New York: Fordham University Press, 2005.

Chappel, Tom. *The Soul of A Business; Managing for Profit and the Common Good.* New York: Bantam Books, 1993.

Csikszentmihalyi, M. *The Evolving Self.* New York: Harper Perennial, 1993.

Dawkins, Richard. *The God Delusion.* New York: Houghton Mifflin Company, 2006.

Dennett, Daniel C. *Breaking the Spell: Religion as a Natural Phenomenon.* New York: Viking, 2006.

Dewey, John. *Art and Experience.* New York: Minton, Balch & Co., 1934.

———. *A Common Faith.* New Haven: Yale University Press, 1934.

———. *The Quest for Certainty.* New York: G. P. Putnam and Sons, 1929.

———. *Individualism: Old and New.* Amherst, NY: Prometheus Books, 1999.

Dewey, John, and James Tufts. *Ethics.* 1908. New York: Henry Hold, 1932.

Enderle, Georges. "Business Ethics and Wealth Creation: Conceptual Clarifications and Research Questions." Department of Business Ethics, University of Notre Dame.

Fowler, George. *Dance of a Fallen Monk: The Twists and Turns of a Spiritual Life.* Reading, MA: Addison-Wesley, 1995.

Friedman, Thomas L. *The World Is Flat: A Brief History of the Twenty-first Century.* New York: Farrar, Straus and Giroux, updated and expanded, 2006.

Fromm, Eric. *On Disobedience and Other Essays.* New York: Seabury Press, 1981.

Gardner, Howard. *Changing Minds.* Boston: Harvard Business School Press, 2004.

Gardner, Howard, Mihaly Csikszentmihalyi, and William Damon. *Good Work: When Excellence and Ethics Meet.* New York: Basic Books, 2001.

Gergen, Kenneth J., Sheila McNamee, and Frank J. Barrett. "Toward Transformative Dialogue." *International Journal of Public Administration* 24, nos. 7 and 8 (2001): 679–707.

Greenberg, Irving. *For the Sake of Heaven and Earth: The New Encounter Between Judaism and Christianity.* Philadelphia: Jewish Publication Society, 2004.

———. *The Jewish Way: Living the Holidays.* New York: Summit Books, 1988.

———. *Living in the Image of God: Jewish Teaching to Perfect the World.* Northvale, NJ: Jason Aronson, 1998.

Grudin, Robert. *On Dialogue.* Boston: Houghton Mifflin, 1996.

Habermas, Jurgen. "Religion in the Public Sphere." *European Journal of Philosophy* 14, no. 1 (2006): 1–25.

Halberstam, Joshua. *Schmoozing: The Private Conversations of American Jews.* New York: Berkley Publishing Group, 1997.

Harris, Sam. *The End of Faith: Religion, Terror, and the Future of Reason.* New York: W. W. Norton & Company, 2004.

Havel, Vaclav. *Summer Meditations.* New York: Alfred Knopf, 1992.

Heifetz, R. A. *Leadership Without Easy Answers.* Cambridge, MA: Harvard University Press, 1994.

Heifetz, R. A., and Linsky, M. *Leadership on the Line.* Boston: Harvard University Press, 2002.

Heschel, Abraham Joshua. *The Sabbath: Its Meaning for Modern Man.* New York: Farrar, Straus and Giroux, 1951.

Hitchens, Christopher. *God is not Great: How Religion Poisons Everything.* New York: Twelve, 2007.

Idel, M. *Kabbalah & Eros.* New Haven, CT: Yale University Press, 2005.

Isaacs, William. *Dialogue and the Art of Thinking Together.* New York: Currency, 1999.

Jackson, Philip W. *John Dewey and the Lessons of Art*. New Haven: Yale University Press, 1998.

James, William. *A Pluralistic Universe*. New York: Longmans, Green, 1909.

———. *Pragmatism*. Buffalo: Prometheus Books, 1991.

———. *The Will to Believe and Other Essays in Popular Philosophy*. New York: Dover, 1956.

Janis, Irving L. "Groupthink Among Policy Makers." In *Sanctions for Evil*, edited by Nevitt Sanford and Craig Comstock, 71–89. San Francisco: Jossey-Bass, 1971. Available at www.er.uqam.ca/nobel/d101000/JanisGroupthinkPolicyMakers.pdf

Jaworski, Joseph. *Synchronicity: The Inner Path of Leadership*. San Francisco: Berrett-Koehler, 1996.

Johnson, Mark. *Moral Imagination: Implication of Cognitive Science for Ethics*. Chicago: University of Chicago Press, 1993.

Kabat-Zinn, Jon. *Coming to Our Senses: Healing the World Through Mindfulness*. New York: Hyperion, 2005.

Kegan, Robert. *The Evolving Self: Problems and Process in Human Development*. Cambridge, MA: Harvard University Press, 1982.

———. *In Over Our Heads: The Mental Demands of Modern Life*. Cambridge, MA: Harvard University Press, 1994.

Kegan, R., and Lahey, L. L. *How the Way We Talk Can Change the Way We Work*. San Francisco: Jossey-Bass, 2001.

Kimelman, Reuven. "Rabbis Joseph B. Soloveitchik and Abraham Joshua Heschel on Jewish-Christian Relations." *The Edah Journal* 4, no. 2 (2004): 1–21.

Korn, Eugene. "The Man of Faith and Religious Dialogue: Revisiting 'Confrontation' After Forty Years." Available at http://www.bc.edu/research/cjl (accessed July 30, 2006).

Lamm, Norman. *Shema: Spirituality and Law in Judaism*. Philadelphia: Jewish Publication Society, 1998.

Leamer, Edward E. "A Flat World, A Level Playing Field, A Small world After All or None of the Above?" Review of *The World Is Flat*, by Thomas L. Friedman. 2006. Available at http://www.international.ucla.edu/research/private/article.asp?parentid=38236

March, James. *The Pursuit of Organizational Intelligence*. Oxford: Blackwell, 1999.

McNamee, Sheila and Kenneth J. Gergen and Associates. *Relational Responsibilities: Resources for Sustainable Dialogue*. Thousand Oaks, CA: Sage, 1999.

Miller, J. *Education and the Soul*. New York: State University of New York Press, 2000.

Mitchell, Steven A. *Can Love Last?*. New York: W. W. Norton, 2002.

Mitroff, Ian, and Elizabeth Denton. *A Spiritual Audit of Corporate America*. San Francisco: Jossey-Bass, 1999.

Nadesan, Majia Holmer. "The Discourses of Corporate Spiritualism and Evangelical Capitalsim." *Management Communication Quarterly* 13, no. 1 (August 1999): 3–42.

Neal, Judi. "Work as Service to the Divine: Giving our Gifts Selflessly and with Joy." *The American Behavioral Scientist* 43, no. 8 (May 2000): 1316–33.

Novak, Michael. "Remembering the Secular Age." *First Things* 174 (June–July 2007). Available at http://www.firstthings.com/article .php3?id_article=5922.

Oppenheim, Michael. "Irving Greenberg and a Jewish Dialectic of Hope." *Judaism* (Spring 2000). Available at http://findarticles.com/p/articles/ mi_m0411/is_2_49/ai_64332271/

Palmer, P. J. *The Courage to Teach.* San Francisco: Jossey-Bass, 1998.

Parks, Sharon Daloz. *Big Questions, Worthy Dreams: Mentoring Young Adults in Their Search for Meaning, Purpose, and Faith.* San Francisco: Jossey-Bass, 2000.

Pava, Moses. *The Jewish Ethics Workbook.* 2005. Available at http://www .edah.org.

———. *Leading With Meaning: Using Covenantal Leadership to Build a Better Organization.* New York: Palgrave, 2003.

———. *The Search for Meaning in Organizations: Seven Practical Questions for Ethical Managers.* Westport, CT: Quorum, 1999.

Peli, Pinchus. *On Repentance.* Jerusalem: Oroth, 1980.

Phillips, Adam. *Promises, Promises: Essays on Psychoanalysis and Literature.* New York: Basic Books, 2001.

Porras, Jerry, and Jim Collins. *Built To Last.* New York: Harper Business, 1994.

Quinn, Robert E. *Building the Bridge as You Walk On It: A Guide For Leading Change.* San Francisco: Jossey-Bass, 2004.

Quinn, Robert, Gretchen Spreitzer, and Matthew Brown. "Changing Others Through Changing Ourselves: The Transformation of Human Systems." *Journal of Management Inquiry* 7, no. 2 (June 2000): 147–64.

Reeve, C. D. C. *Love's Confusions.* Cambridge, MA: Harvard University Press, 2004.

Rockefeller, Stephen C. *John Dewey: Religious Faith and Democratic Humanism* New York: Columbia University Press, 1991.

Sacks, Jonathan. *To Heal a Fractured World.* London: Continuum, 2005.

Seeskin, Kenneth. *Searching for a Distant God: The Legacy of Maimonides.* New York: Oxford University Press, 2000.

Shotter, John. *Conversational Realities: Constructing Life Through Language.* London: Sage, 2002.

Singer, Irving. *The Creation of Value.* Baltimore: Johns Hopkins University Press, 1992.

Solomon, Robert C. *Spirituality for the Skeptic: The Thoughtful Love of Life.* Oxford: Oxford University Press, 2002.

Soloveitchik, Joseph B. "Confrontation." *Tradition* 5, no. 2 (1964). Available at http://www.bc.edu/research/cjl/meta-elements/texts/cjrelations/resources/articles/soloveitchik/

———. *The Lonely Man of Faith.* New York: Doubleday, 1965.

Stiglitz, Joseph E. "Evaluating Economic Change." *Daedalus* 133, no. 3 (Summer 2004): 18–25.

Stout, Jeffrey. *Ethics After Babel.* Princeton, NJ: Princeton University Press, 1988.

Taylor, Charles. *Ethics of Authenticity.* Cambridge, MA: Harvard University Press, 1991.

———. *The Sources of Self: The Making of Modern Identity.* Cambridge, MA: Harvard University Press, 1989.

Tonn, Mari Boor. "Taking Conversation, Dialogue, and Therapy Public." *Rhetoric and Public Affairs* 8, no. 3 (2005): 405–30.

Twersky, Isadore. *A Maimonides Reader.* Springfield, NJ: Library of Jewish Studies, 1972.

Unerman, Jeffrey, and Mark Bennett. "Increased Stakeholder Dialogue and the Internet: Towards Greater Corporate Accountability or Reinforcing Capitalist Hegemony?" *Accounting Organizations and Society* 29 (2004): 685–707.

Unger, R. M. *Passion: An Essay on Personality.* New York: Free Press, 1984.

Walzer, Michael. *On Toleration.* New Haven, CT: Yale University Press, 1997.

Wheatley, Margaret J. *Turning to One Another: Simple Conversations to Restore Hope to the Future.* San Francisco: Berrett-Koehler, 2002.

Wilber, Ken. *The Marriage of Sense and Soul: Integrating Science and Religion.* New York: Broadway Books, 1998.

Woodruff, Paul. *Reverence: Renewing a Forgotten Virtue.* New York: Oxford University Press, 2001.

Wuthnow, Robert. *Poor Richard's Principle: Recovering the American Dream Through the Moral Dimension of Work, Business & Money.* Princeton, NJ: Princeton University Press, 1996.

Index